Cambridge Elements ☰

Elements in Business Strategy
edited by
J.-C. Spender
Rutgers Business School

MICROFOUNDATIONS

Nature, Debate, and Promise

Nicolai J. Foss
Bocconi University

Stefan Linder
ESSEC Business School

CAMBRIDGE
UNIVERSITY PRESS

CAMBRIDGE
UNIVERSITY PRESS

University Printing House, Cambridge CB2 8BS, United Kingdom

One Liberty Plaza, 20th Floor, New York, NY 10006, USA

477 Williamstown Road, Port Melbourne, VIC 3207, Australia

314–321, 3rd Floor, Plot 3, Splendor Forum, Jasola District Centre,
New Delhi – 110025, India

79 Anson Road, #06–04/06, Singapore 079906

Cambridge University Press is part of the University of Cambridge.

It furthers the University's mission by disseminating knowledge in the pursuit of
education, learning, and research at the highest international levels of excellence.

www.cambridge.org
Information on this title: www.cambridge.org/9781108468985
DOI: 10.1017/9781108685498

© Nicolai J. Foss and Stefan Linder 2019

First published 2019

A catalogue record for this publication is available from the British Library.

ISBN 978-1-108-46898-5 Paperback
ISSN 2515-0693 (online)
ISSN 2515-0685 (print)

Microfoundations

Nature, Debate, and Promise

Elements in Business Strategy

DOI: 10.1017/9781108685498
First published online: November 2019

Nicolai J. Foss
Bocconi University

Stefan Linder
ESSEC Business School

Author for correspondence: Nicolai J. Foss, nicolai.foss@unibocconi.it

Abstract: 'Microfoundations' has become prominent in the discourse of management scholars. But what is it and how does it matter? This Element provides a characterization of microfoundations based on classical work on the methodology of social science and documents and discusses its manifestations in management research over the last one and a half decades. It also covers the relation of microfoundations to multilevel research; criticisms of microfoundations; and empirical research strategies for microfoundations.

Keywords: management; methodological individualism; microfoundations; research methodology; strategy

ISBNs: 9781108468985 (PB), 9781108685498 (OC)
ISSNs: 2515-0693 (online), 2515-0685 (print)

Contents

1 Introduction

'Microfoundations' has become something of a buzzword in management theory. It is frequently heard at the major management or themed conferences, featured in special issues of leading journals, invoked at research seminars, and increasingly figures in headings of papers in the top-rated management journals.

This is a quite recent development. Fifteen years ago, there was no mention of microfoundations in the management literature.[1] The 'microfoundations movement', as Winter (2013) called it, has swept across the management theory landscape over the past decade (see also Aguinis and Molina-Azorin, 2015). The 'opening salvo' stating the microfoundations position in management, namely Felin and Foss (2005), was primarily an attack on what these authors saw as an excessive use of macro constructs without clear microfoundations, such as routines, capabilities, absorptive capacity, and the like. Felin and Foss argued that it was basically unclear how a construct such as (firm-level) 'capability' relates to the skills, knowledge, actions, and interactions of organizational members.[2] In other words, 'capability' was a construct with unclear microfoundations. This was a major problem for various influential views in strategy that postulated a link between firm-level capabilities and firm performance, seemingly without paying any attention to the role of individuals. But capabilities matter to the extent that they represent the ability to somehow mobilize (coordinate, incentivize) the resources and services that are involved in production, including the human resources (HR) of organizational members (Abell, Felin, and Foss, 2008). Thus, the point of Felin and Foss (2005) was not to eliminate macro (or 'collective-level') constructs in management theory, but to make scholars aware of the need to clarify their microfoundations.[3]

Building microfoundations for macro constructs is not just a lofty, theoretical problem. If a manager does not understand how the capabilities of the firm she manages somehow emerge from individual-level skills, actions, and so on, it is not clear how she can manage capabilities, including developing and leveraging such capabilities. In other words, microfoundations matter also for practical reasons.

Clearly, the attack resonated with many and may have given further impetus to developments that were already under way. For example, there is now work

---

[1] The discussion of microfoundations in other disciplines and fields is considerably older. For those who seek good, relatively non-technical general expositions of microfoundations and thinking on methodological individualism, we highly recommend Hodgson (2007), Janssen (2005) (which deals specifically with economics), Little (1998), and Udehn (2001, 2002).

[2] Spender (1996) raised similar concerns, but without endorsing microfoundations.

[3] However, see Felin and Hesterly (2007) for the more radical position that firm capabilities may simply be epiphenomena of individuals, specifically individuals of similar ability selecting into the same firms.

on the microfoundations of routines, institutional logics, absorptive capacity, stakeholder management, innovation, ambidexterity, networks, organizational capabilities, sustainability capabilities, and dynamic capabilities (e.g., Bapuji, Hora, and Saeed, 2012; Bridoux and Stoelhorst, 2014; Cohen, 2012; Grigoriou and Rothaermel, 2014; Helfat and Peteraf, 2015; Morris, Hammond, and Snell, 2014; Strauss, Lepoutre, and Wood, 2017; Teece, 2007; Thornton, Ocasio, and Lounsbury, 2012). However, the relatively aggressive tone of Felin and Foss (2005; see also Felin and Foss, 2011) also alienated some scholars (e.g., Hodgson, 2012; Pentland, 2011; Winter, 2011). Indeed, the microfoundations movement has been charged with trying to smuggle the rational choice model of economics into management theory and for implying that macro constructs are meaningless (charges that are incorrect).

But what is it all about? The purpose of this slim volume is to provide an introduction to this influential current in contemporary management thought. We focus on the key features of 'microfoundations' and how it differs from other currents, its promises for advancing management theory, and the points voiced against it, and some recent applications.

A key point that we will elaborate in greater detail is that 'microfoundations' is not a theory, such as the resource-based theory in strategy, agency theory in economics, or self-determination theory in psychology and human resource management (HRM). (In fact, because misconceptions are prevalent, there will be quite a bit of 'microfoundations are not' in this volume.) Rather, *it is a way to think of how to explain social phenomena, and a set of concomitant structuring and modelling heuristics. These are part of an attempt to unpack collective (or 'macro') concepts and phenomena so to foster improved understanding of them.*

Thus, microfoundations may be seen as part of the reductionist quest of science, that is, the idea that understanding, explanation, and ultimately prediction is furthered by decomposing collective phenomena to the cogs and wheels, the mechanisms and the entities involved in such mechanisms, which produce them. To put it differently, microfoundations opens 'black boxes' – that is, the parts of an explanation that we deem important to a full, satisfactory explanation, but do not grasp so far. In a nutshell, microfoundations seek to foster this understanding by explaining how micro-level factors like individuals' characteristics, their decision-rights, their interactions, and so on impact meso- and macro-level outcomes – for example, how the interaction of individuals leads to emergent, collective, and organization-level outcomes (e.g., an organization's goals, strategy, performance etc.) – and how relations between macro variables, such as, for example, between firm strategy and firm performance, are mediated by micro actions and interactions (e.g., Abell, Felin, and Foss, 2008).

We and many others believe that microfoundations offer the potential to significantly enhance our understanding of phenomena in management, business, and society more generally. Nevertheless, the microfoundations current is not greeted with enthusiasm by all (Devinney, 2013). Some have flatly questioned the value added of microfoundations for macro fields in management, such as strategy, international business, organization, innovation management, and the like (e.g., Hodgson, 2012; Jacobides and Winter, 2012; Winter, 2012a). Others in turn have argued that the microfoundations notion unnecessarily valourizes individual-level agency over social context and process (Jepperson and Meyer, 2011) or simply recycles insights from micro disciplines and fields (e.g., psychology or organizational behaviour (OB)) (see Barney and Felin, 2013). Discussions about microfoundations therefore have a tendency to turn (degenerate?) into discussions about 'reductionism' and 'methodological individualism', both of which are not entirely uncontroversial positions. We touch on these discussions and mention some of these issues (e.g., on the nature of inter- and intra-level relations, the ontological status of levels, etc.).[4]

The emphasis of this volume is thus on thinking microfoundationally about management research issues. Where does thinking promise to advance our understanding? How is it done? What insights have already been generated by the microfoundations movement? This also means that our intended audience is not philosophers or specialists in the methodology of social science (or management), but bright master-level students, PhD students in social science and management, and management academics and consultants seeking an update on an influential contemporary current in management thought.[5]

We start off in Section 2 with an example from the strategy literature to illustrate what microfoundations are and how microfoundations can help advance our understanding. Subsequently, we offer an overview of recent

---

[4] However, it is important to stress that, even though microfoundations do seem to us to imply a weak form of reductionism, they do not necessarily involve methodological individualism. Moreover, a weak form of reduction of complexity can sometimes facilitate studying certain relations and, hence, be one way to advance our knowledge, or as Nelson and Winter (1982: 134) put it: 'theorists should aim to tell the truth in their theorizing, but they cannot aim to tell the whole truth. For to theorize is precisely to focus on those entities and relationships in reality that are believed to be central to the phenomenon observed – and largely ignore the rest.'

[5] This Element draws on various published material, notably Abell, Felin, and Foss (2008), Felin and Foss (2005, 2006), and Felin et al. (2012), as well as Felin, Foss, and Ployhart (2015). Thus, there is substantial thematic overlap with these papers. The volume also draws on various exchanges and debates with colleagues that we have had in recent years as well as on a working paper by Abell, Foss, and Lyngsie (Empirical microfoundations for management research. Copenhagen: Department of Strategic Management and Globalization, Copenhagen Business School). Yet, the present volume integrates these insights, conditions it for the intended audience, updates the review offered in Felin, Foss, and Ployhart (2015), and extends earlier publications in several ways.

microfoundational work within management research. The overview draws on the systematic review approach suggested by Denyer and Tranfield (2008) and extends earlier work published in Felin, Foss, and Ployhart (2015). This leads us to discuss the promises of microfoundations work.

In Section 3 we delve deeper into the concept of microfoundations, the different interpretations of the nature of microfoundations – namely 'microfoundations as a levels argument' and 'microfoundations as bringing individuals back in' – and discuss the structure of microfoundational explanations, including multiperiod explanations and aspects of granularity of explanations. Subsequently, in Section 4 we turn to the criticisms voiced against the microfoundations movement and discuss concerns, like, for example, that microfoundations are simply reinventing and relabelling extant research in organizational behaviour (OB) or human resource management (HRM).

Section 5 is dedicated to the empirical dimension of microfoundations. Thus, it provides a short overview and discussion of various empirical methods and approaches that seem promising for microfoundations research, but also discusses the particular challenges that microfoundations raise for empirical research.

Finally, in Section 6 we end with a reflection and discussion of the role of microfoundations for fostering theory-building, enhancing management education and business practice, and how microfoundations can be made more alive both theoretically and empirically.

2 Microfoundations in Recent Management Research

2.1 What Are Microfoundations? Examples and a First Sketch

Although microfoundations have been discussed in several management fields, the strategy field arguably is where the discussion has been most intense. Strategy also naturally lends itself to illustrating what microfoundations are by means of examples. Let's therefore consider a, and perhaps *the*, key concept of the strategy field, namely *firm performance*.

Beyond strategy, firm performance is of high and obvious interest to many practitioners and scholars in economics and management. Not surprisingly, what drives or influences such performance has attracted substantial research efforts over the past decades. This has led to various perspectives and theories for explaining them, such as, among the more prominent ones, the structure-conduct-performance (SCP) theory in industrial economics and its applications in strategy (e.g., Bain, 1959; Porter, 1979; Scherer, 1980) and the resource-based view (RBV) (e.g., Barney, 1991; Peteraf and Barney, 2003; Wernerfelt, 1984), or the upper-echelons perspective (beginning with Hambrick and Mason, 1984), which highlights the importance of top-manager characteristics for understanding firm behaviour and, ultimately, performance. As the reader may have guessed, these are not random picks among the many theories we could have chosen.

Whereas all these theories and perspectives seek to explain the same construct, that is, firm performance, they do so by invoking different 'levels' of analysis and mechanisms that are operative at these levels (and across levels). Thus, the SCP theory focuses on industry-level characteristics (mainly 'structure', hence, the 'S') and how they affect firm performance (the 'P') by influencing the behaviour (or 'conduct') of the various firms in a focal industry (Scherer, 1980). The RBV (Barney, 1991), in turn, highlights instead the resources controlled by a firm, which, it is asserted, are comparatively neglected in industrial economics. The focus of the RBV is on how the characteristics of those resources (in terms of being valuable, rare, and costly to imitate and substitute) drive performance. Finally, the upper-echelons' perspective looks at how the 'background characteristics' (Hambrick and Mason, 1984: 193), such as gender, age, experience, or personality traits, of the firm's top managers influence the firm's actions and performance.

Among these three exemplary theories and perspectives, the SCP theory clearly is the one that looks at the phenomenon of firm performance on the most 'macro' level of the three by highlighting factors of the industry structure (it says very little about what is 'inside' the firm). The upper-echelons' perspective, in turn, is among these theories looking at the phenomenon from the most 'micro'-level perspective. The RBV spans levels to some extent, as it includes resources that are basically firm-level resources (e.g., corporate culture) as well as, for example, the human capital embodied in managers (or employees).

The three theories and perspectives thus differ in the level of analysis used for studying the phenomenon, but all can point to empirical work that supports their respective takes on the causes of firm performance. They thus highlight that firm performance like many other (if not most) phenomena of interest to scholars and practitioners, is a phenomenon the causes of which span several levels of analysis, from the micro-level of, say, a particularly talented CEO to the macro-level of, say, a particularly attractive industry. Indeed, these causes may be related (e.g., the talented CEO made the firm diversify into the attractive industry). Not only the causes of key phenomena like performance may be placed at multiple levels; the phenomena *themselves* may span levels of analysis. Thus, a construct such as a routine or a firm capability may be something we would intuitively place at the macro (firm) level. We may indeed think of the representation of the routine in, for example, a set of instructions as existing separately from the individuals that execute the routine, but the actual carrying out of the routine is constituted by a set of sequential actions carried out by organizational members. Thus, in actuality routine performance spans the individual and the organizational levels.

The microfoundations approach fully recognizes that many, if not all, economic and business phenomena are multilevel (with the term 'level' referring to where a particular phenomenon, construct, or process is situated in an ontological sense, not necessarily within an organizational hierarchy; see Felin, Foss, and Ployhart, 2015). It thus is compatible with most modern research in management that highlights the role of individual, small group, subunit, organizational, and inter-organizational levels for understanding social phenomena (e.g., Haas and Cummings, 2015; Hitt et al., 2007; Humphrey and LeBreton, 2019; Mathieu and Chen, 2011). Lower levels are nested within higher levels and the highest, lowest, and number and nature of intermediate levels varies with the scholarly question of interest (Molloy, Ployhart, and Wright, 2011). Thus, for example, the 'micro-level' for a particular industry- or ecosystem-wide ('macro') development, such as digitalization, could well be the individual firms in a particular industry if one is interested in understanding how digitalization affects competition in the industry. It thus does not necessarily have to be the individual manager or employee within these firms, but the individual firm would suffice (at least in the reading of 'microfoundations as levels' perspective – more on this later). At the same time, however, if the phenomenon of interest is individual firms' innovation or adaptive behaviours (i.e., the firm is the 'macro'), then it may well merit going 'further down' in the ontological levels, for example, to the level of the top management team (TMT) and how its decisions are affected by digitalization ('micro') and how their decisions then shape the firm-level actions.

Of course, the very concept of 'microfoundations' signals this: something is the 'foundation', at a 'micro' level, for something else, at a higher, 'macro' level. For example, a possible microfoundational claim could be that ultimately all the industry-level determinants of firm performance identified in industrial economics can be reduced to what individuals believe, think, do, and so on and how they interact. In fact, economics does subscribe to such a claim, even if it may not always be that transparent.

A basic assumption of the microfoundations approach is that knowledge is often advanced by means of reductive operations. This is no different from the common idea in science that 'reduction is at the heart of scientific progress' (Elster, 1989: 74).[6] Coleman (1990: chapter 1) explains that reducing macro-phenomena to its constituent microcomponents yields additional insight because macro-level

---

[6] As Felin et al. (2012: 1354) argue, '[s]cientific reduction is a call for explaining collective phenomena and structures in terms of what are seen as more fundamental, nested components (Kincaid, 1997) and the search for, and explication of, the constituent components that underlie aggregate and collective phenomena'.

explanation (i.e., explanation of macro phenomena in terms of other macro phenomena) cannot discriminate between the many potential alternative lower-level explanations of macro-level behaviour because of a fundamental problem of unobserved mechanisms.[7] Moreover, as Felin et al. (2015: 583) outline, various macro, social, or relational constructs, such as networks, 'might simply be epiphenomena or artefacts of lower-level antecedents, rather than key variables that explain theoretically or empirically'. Being in a structural hole, or being a central broker in a network, or possessing particular ties, as they explain, might have to do with the characteristics of the nodes, thus not allowing scholars to make assumptions of node or individual homogeneity. Reductive operations, thus, can help disentangle key variables from artefacts. Finally, from the perspective of business practice and advising business practitioners, such reductive operations facilitate intervening in macro phenomena as they point to the most proximate causes, that is, the levers that individual managers and firms can pull.[8]

Accordingly, the microfoundations project in social science and, therefore, also in management seeks to advance our understanding of phenomena by ensuring that analysis explicitly considers this multilevel nature by locating (theoretically and empirically) the proximate causes of the phenomenon one seeks to explain at one or more levels of analysis lower than that of the phenomenon itself. For example, as Felin et al. (2012) explain, the actions of a cartel may be explained in terms of the actions of the participating firms, or the functioning of a firm-internal routine may be explained in terms of the coordinated actions of individuals. Similarly, a firm's dynamic capabilities can be explained, as Teece (2007) maintains, by 'the distinct skills, processes, procedures, organizational structures, decision rules, and disciplines ... which undergird enterprise-level sensing, seizing, and reconfiguring of capacities that are difficult to develop and deploy' (Teece 2007: 1319).

As these examples suggest, microfoundations understood as what Felin et al. (2012) call the 'microfoundations as levels' argument may or may not directly involve individuals. Reducing higher-level entities to the actions and interactions of lower-level entities is, strictly speaking, a microfoundational operation. Of course, a proponent of methodological individualism – the position that

---

[7] For example, the capabilities view seeks the explanation of differential firm performance in firm-level heterogeneity, that is, heterogeneous routines and capabilities. However, heterogeneity may be located at the individual level, notably when individuals self-select into particular firms (Felin and Hesterly, 2007).

[8] For example, it makes little sense to argue that managers can directly intervene on the level of, for example, capabilities. Perhaps, however, managers can *influence* capabilities, for example, by hiring key employees, changing organizational structure, implementing new forms of training, control, information and communication, engaging in symbolic acts, and so on. To the extent that such managerial choices influence capabilities, it is because they influence the abilities, motivation, and opportunities of organizational members.

ultimately all macro phenomena can and should be reduced to actions and interactions of individuals – will argue that such microfoundations are at best preliminary to the eventual reduction to the level of individuals. We will get to methodological individualism in a moment, and here note two broader points. First, microfoundations do not mean that collective constructs and macro variables have no place in explanation (Felin, Foss, and Ployhart, 2015; Little, 1991). Second, microfoundations may not only be flexible with respect to what is 'micro', but also with respect to what is 'macro': in the examples, cartels, routines, and dynamic capabilities can all be taken to be 'macro' although they are in actuality placed at different levels of analysis (routines and dynamic capabilities as characteristics of a firm and cartels as gatherings of several firms).

In addition to the interpretation of microfoundations as a levels argument, an interpretation of microfoundations as the 'explanatory primacy of individuals' also exist. This is the interpretation of microfoundations-as-methodological individualism. This position goes back at least to the Scottish Enlightenment, that is, philosophers and social scientists such as David Hume, Adam Smith, Adam Ferguson, and others. They highlighted those human institutions that are the 'results of human action, not of human design' (see Hayek, 1973), and offered 'conjectural history' that was based on this basic idea. Thus, Smith and Hume both told 'stories' about how key societal institutions, notably that of property, may plausibly have emerged in a spontaneous manner, given the universal facts of scarcity and self-interest, thus explicitly starting from assumptions about individuals. Methodological individualism was revived by the Austrian School of Economics towards the end of the nineteenth century (Menger, 1883 [1985]), restated by Karl Popper and other philosophers, and today is one of the key basic assumptions of virtually all of economics. This interpretation is clearly more contestable than the interpretation of microfoundations as a levels argument, and also more specific (this interpretation may be seen as a special case of the microfoundations as a levels argument). It is this more specific interpretation that also has sparked much of the criticism voiced against the 'microfoundations movement', as some critics have feared that microfoundations means smuggling in economics assumptions rather through the back door.

However, while the 'microfoundations project' (Winter, 2011) is indeed committed to a kind of reductionism, it is not necessarily committed to methodological individualism and it is certainly not committed to the behavioural assumptions that are characteristic of economics. The basic commitment of the microfoundations project is probably to a layered ontology of social reality[9]–

---

[9] This assumption is not philosophically uncontroversial. An alternative ontology is that the social world is flat rather than hierarchical, but that scaling matters (e.g., small-scale vs large-scale situations).

one that has the economy at the top, followed by industry, firms, units within firms, groups of individuals, and with individuals at the bottom (Little, 1998). And both the 'microfoundations as levels' and the 'microfoundations as explanatory primacy of individuals' view – assert that all explanations of higher-level phenomena should depart from lower-level phenomena or actors as the proximate causes. Or, as Felin, Foss, and Ployhart (2015: 587) argue, at the very least 'lower level factors should be controlled for (rather than simply assuming that the lower level is homogeneous)'. To stay in our example, firm performance clearly is a firm-level (here: macro-level) construct. There is no strategy field without such constructs as firm performance, value creation, and competitive advantage, which all are firm-level constructs, that is, on a level higher than that of the individual. What the microfoundations movement submits is that scientific progress requires scholars to know how lower-level phenomena or actors as the proximate causes influence these firm-level constructs.

It thus cautions against work that 'stays at the surface' by first introducing firm-level constructs that do not have clear microfoundations, and, second, seeking to establish causal relations between macro (organizational) variables, as in arguments that certain macro-features of a firm somehow directly cause superior performance, with individuals and groups of individuals playing no discernible role in such stories. As microfoundations thus implies a quest for a multilevel explanation that privileges the lower-level and is concerned with how causality unfolds between and within levels in terms of mechanisms, it is not surprising that microfoundations in research practice may mean methodological individualism.

Yet, how thus do scholars use the microfoundations lens in management research? For example, how much of the flexibility of microfoundations with respect to what is 'micro' and what is 'macro' do they use? How many follow a 'microfoundations as levels', and how many a 'microfoundations as explanatory primacy of individuals' perspective? In the following section, we present an overview of recent microfoundational work within management research drawing on the systematic review approach suggested by Denyer and Tranfield (2008) and extending earlier work published in Felin, Foss, and Ployhart (2015).

2.2 The Microfoundations Movement: A Look at the Journals

Whereas the microfoundations movement arguable enjoys most popularity within the strategy field, there increasingly is now work invoking the notion of microfoundations in the management literature more generally. Some time ago, Felin, Foss, and Ployhart (2015) offered an extensive overview of microfoundational work in the management literature published up to 2014, which helps understand the multiple versions in which microfoundations come along and illustrates the broad spectrum of phenomena to which they have been applied. Yet, given the growing popularity of microfoundations, quite a number of additional publications have come out since 2014. We therefore searched the literature and in following present an updated and extended version of the Felin et al. (2015) overview.

Method

Our overview draws on the systematic review approach suggested by Denyer and Tranfield (2008) and covers articles published in the *Academy of Management Review, Academy of Management Journal, Administrative Science Quarterly, Journal of Business Research, Journal of International Business Studies, Journal of Management, Journal of Management Studies, Long Range Planning, Management Science, Organization Science,* and *Strategic Management Journal* from 2003 until 2017. Obviously, a search limited to these journals can pick up only on a subset of the work employing a microfoundations lens. It abstracts from research published in books or book chapters or in other journals. However, our objective here is not to catalogue every work that mentions 'micro(-)foundation(s)'. Rather, we offer a snapshot picture of the breadth of microfoundations work published in some of the main and most influential outlets in management research. We believe that such a picture helps get a better understanding of the microfoundations movement, topics that the microfoundations lens has been profitably applied to, and the multiple versions in which microfoundations come along.

Before we turn to these points, here is how we did the review. We relied on three keywords, namely 'microfoundations', 'microfoundational', and 'methodological individualism'. Any keyword-based search risks overlooking work that does not use the particular keywords chosen; however, these three keywords are likely to pick up most publications with a microfoundations spirit as they are arguably the ones most commonly used. The keyword-based search covered article titles, abstracts, and author-provided keywords of the articles. For the resulting list of articles, we subsequently checked whether the articles indeed are examples of microfoundational work. Like in Felin et al. (2015), the criterion for including articles was whether the article in question explicitly seeks to establish relations between analytical levels, in some fashion privileging the most micro-level (as previously explained). Consequently, like in Felin et al. (2015), articles on multilevel modelling are not included in the subsequent overview if they do not specifically put an emphasis on any particular (lower) level of analysis.

Findings

Table 1[10] provides a summary of key articles published in these thirteen top journals, which are explicitly positioned as microfoundational contributions.

The first article explicitly mentioning microfoundations in a highly ranked (macro-) management journal, the *Strategic Management Journal* (Lippman and Rumelt, 2003a) does not present a general case for microfoundations. However, Lippman and Rumelt (2003a) make the important point that there is no aggregate, firm-level return called 'profits' that is appropriated by an entity called the firm. Accounting conventions, the law, and established theory may convey this impression. But, in actuality there is no independent entity called 'the firm' that appropriates profits. Payments are nominally made by buyers to the firm (a legal fiction), but the firm constitutes managers, employees, and owners. Also, (legally independent) suppliers obtain payments from the firm. In the end, all 'firm-level profits' are paid to the owners of the resources, the services of which enter into firm operations. How much each resource owner is paid depends on a complex process of bargaining. In turn, expected payments influences the willingness of resource owners to contribute services to the firm. Note how all these points are fundamentally microfoundational ones: they involve reducing an aggregate, and potentially misleading, notion – that is, the notion that 'firms appropriate profits' – into something more fine-grained. Also note that additional insights are being obtained in the process, notably into bargaining among resource owners and how such bargaining influences incentives to contribute effort to the firm and engage in relation-specific investments.

However, as our literature search demonstrations, it was not until after 2010 that explicitly microfoundational work became popular in terms of the number of published papers in the thirteen top journals surveyed. Moreover, the relatively few works that were published prior to 2010 were largely conceptual and theoretical. Empirical research explicitly mentioning microfoundations is a very recent development. (We later discuss the challenges that may explain why it is a relatively late development.)

Much of the extant work on microfoundations addresses those areas of management research that stress 'knowledge-based' assets, for example, routines, capabilities, competences, absorptive capacity, human capital

---

[10] This table is an updated and extended version of the table published in Felin, Foss, and Ployhart (2015).

Table 1 Key microfoundational work 2003–17[11]

Articles (chronologically arranged)	Understanding of microfoundations	Explanandum	Explanans	Method
Lippman and Rumelt (2003a)	Bargaining outcomes understood in terms of the bargaining behaviours of individual resource owners	Resource-level value appropriation	Bargaining strengths of individual resource owners	Conceptual and theoretical
Lippman and Rumelt (2003b)	'The microfoundations of a subject are the definitions of its basic elements and the allowable operations that can be performed using these elements' (p. 903)	Rent	Strategies that increase resource scarcity	Conceptual and theoretical
Felin and Hesterly (2007)	Methodological individualism	Firm-level knowledge (e.g., capabilities)	Individual-level heterogeneity	Conceptual and theoretical
Gottschalg and Zollo (2007)	Individual motivation is crucial to understanding organizational outcomes	Value and rent-creation at the individual level	Different kinds of motivation	Conceptual and theoretical
Teece (2007)	'[T]he distinct skills, processes, procedures, organizational structures, decision rules, and disciplines –which undergird enterprise-level sensing, seizing, and reconfiguring capacities' (p. 1319)	Dynamic capabilities	Routines for sensing and seizing opportunities in the environment and reconfiguring assets	Conceptual and theoretical

[11] As of 1 November 2017, based on a search in *Academy of Management Review*, *Academy of Management Journal*, *Administrative Science Quarterly*, *Journal of Business Research*, *Journal of International Business Studies*, *Journal of Management*, *Journal of Management Studies*, *Long Range Planning*, *Management Science*, *Organization Science*, *Research Policy*, *Strategic Management Journal*, and *Strategic Management Journal*. This table draws on Felin, Foss, and Ployhart (2015).

Study	Definition	Level of analysis	Micro-foundation	Method
Nickerson and Zenger (2008)	Organizational phenomena are explainable in terms of individual action and interaction and ultimately in terms of human cognition and affect	Organizational structure	Individual emotions	Conceptual and theoretical
Aime, Johnson, and Ridge (2010)	Not explicitly defined	Competitive advantage	Employee mobility	Analysis of panel data set
Eisenhardt et al. (2010)	'The underlying individual-level and group-level actions that shape strategy, organization, and, more broadly, dynamic capabilities' (p. 1263)	Dynamic capabilities/firm performance	Leadership actions aimed at balancing efficiency and innovation	Conceptual and theoretical
Harrison, Bosse, and Philips (2010)	Not explicitly defined	Firm-level value creation	Organizational justice, which allows more fine-grained managerial access to employee utility functions	Conceptual and theoretical
Lewin, Massini, and Peeters (2011)	Not explicitly defined	Absorptive capacity capabilities	Routines and practices, such as open office plans, brainstorming sessions, and cross-functional project teams	Conceptual and theoretical.
Lindenberg and Foss (2011)	Methodological individualism	Joint production motivation	Intertwined cognition and motivation that is influenced by organizational antecedents	Conceptual and theoretical

Table 1 (cont.)

Articles (chronologically arranged)	Understanding of microfoundations	Explanandum	Explanans	Method
Argote and Ren (2012)	Not explicitly defined	Dynamic capabilities	Transactive memory systems	Conceptual and theoretical.
Bapuji, Hora, and Saeed (2012)	Not explicitly defined	Routines	'Intermediaries' bridge actions and ease routine formation	Field experiment of a towel-charging routine in a hotel
Miller, Pentland, and Choi (2012)	Not explicitly defined	The formation, efficiency, and adaptability of organizational routines	Procedural, declarative, and transactive memory	Agent-based simulation
Mollick (2012)	'[T]he part that individual firm members play in explaining the variance in performance among firms' (p. 1001)	Heterogeneity in firm performance	Relative contribution to firm performance of middle-managers versus inventors	Multilevel empirics
Mäkelä et al. (2012)	Individual action is the foundation of organizational phenomena	Organization-level strategic HRM capabilities	The experience of subsidiary HR managers; and the social capital between managers working with HR issues in the subsidiary and those in the corporate HR function	Analysis of survey data from Nordic multinational corporations

Author (year)	Definition	Phenomenon	Concept	Method
Paruchuri and Eisenman (2012)	Not explicitly defined	How research and development capabilities change following a merger	Inventor networks	Case studies
Pentland et al. (2012)	Not explicitly defined	Routine change	Higher-level routines	Simulation
Baer, Dirks, and Nickerson (2013)	Not explicitly defined	The formulation of strategic problems	Heterogeneous information sets, objectives, and cognitive structures	Conceptual and theoretical
Bridoux and Stoelhorst (2014)	Not explicitly defined	Attracting, retaining, and motivating stakeholders to create value	Stakeholders with different motives who require different types of stakeholder management	Conceptual and theoretical
Grigoriou and Rothaermel (2014)	Organizational phenomena can be reduced to individual action and interaction; however, the 'embeddedness' of individual action must be considered	Knowledge-based organizational advantage (innovation)	Individuals in knowledge networks who are very high in centrality and bridging behaviours	Network analysis
Helfat and Peteraf (2015)	How the cognition of individual managers translate into actions that influence organizational outcomes	Dynamic capabilities	Managerial cognitive capability	Conceptual and theoretical
Miller, Choi, and Pentland (2014)	Not explicitly defined	Routines	Transactive memory	Theoretical and empirical
Morris, Hammond, and Snell (2014)	Not explicitly defined	Transnational capabilities	Diverse knowledge from individuals	Theoretical and empirical

Table 1 (cont.)

Articles (chronologically arranged)	Understanding of microfoundations	Explanandum	Explanans	Method
Rogan and Mors (2014)	Organizational phenomena can be reduced to individual action and interaction	Ambidexterity at the level of individuals. Organization-level implications discussed; however, no explicit aggregation is undertaken in the paper	Characteristics of managers' networks and ties	Network analysis of the internal and external ties of seventy-nine senior managers
Ebers and Maurer (2014)	Not explicitly defined	Absorptive capacity	Boundary spanners' internal and external relational embeddedness and empowerment	Theoretical and empirical
Obloj and Zemsky (2015)	Not explicitly defined	Value creation and division of value in contracting relationships	Supplier heterogeneity	Conceptual and theoretical
Bitektine and Haack (2015)	Not explicitly defined	Organizational legitimacy	Individual's perceptions, judgements, and actions under different organizational conditions	Conceptual and theoretical

Study	Definition	Focus	Description	Type
Chadwick and Raver (2015)	Not explicitly defined	Organizational learning	Heterogeneity of individuals' goal orientations, and their interrelations with group composition and leadership, organizational structure, and resource competition	Conceptual and theoretical
Kim et al. (2016)	Not explicitly defined	Network formation	Firm-level characteristics	Theoretical and empirical
Martinkenaite and Breunig (2016)	Not explicitly defined	Firm-level absorptive capacity	Individual actions and interactions of individual and organizational antecedents based on processes of learning	Conceptual and theoretical
Maak, Pless, and Voegtlin (2016)	Not explicitly defined	Political corporate social responsibility	CEO leadership styles and moderating factors, such as an individual's cognitive and social complexity, and corporate governance	Conceptual and theoretical
Raffiee and Coff (2016)	Not explicitly defined	Firm-specific human capital as a source of sustained competitive advantage	Heterogeneity in individuals' organizational commitment and tenure; employer provided on-the-job training	Theoretical and empirical (empirics, although not multilevel)
Dai et al. (2016)	How individuals, their social relationships, and interactions influence firm-level behaviours, processes, and strategies	An organization's entrepreneurial orientation	Venture teams' transactive memory, intra-team trust, and venture's structural organicity	Theoretical and empirical drawing on 148 firms in China

Table 1 (cont.)

Articles (chronologically arranged)	Understanding of microfoundations	Explanandum	Explanans	Method
Aggarwal, Posen, and Workiewicz (2017)	How individual behaviours interact and aggregate to generate macro-level phenomena	Heterogeneity in adaptive capacity across organizations	Strength of beliefs of individuals in the aggregate; types of technological change	Computational model
Bridoux, Coeurderoy, and Durand (2017)	Not explicitly defined but considered to be 'microfoundations that avoid the pitfall of methodological individualism' (p. 1769)	Firm performance and capabilities development as the result of social interactions at the group level	Heterogeneity in individual social motives to social interactions; heterogeneity in motivational levers at firm level	Conceptual and theoretical
Morris et al. (2017)	Not explicitly defined	Differences in incentive systems between senior executives and employees; Differences in value appropriation	Individual firm-specific human capital investments and current employer's organizational context	Conceptual and theoretical
Yao and Chang (2017)	Not explicitly defined	Absorptive capacity	Heterogeneity in individuals' learning goal orientation and civic virtue	Theoretical and empirical drawing on data from 871 employees from 139 firms

Tuncdogan et al. (2017)	Not explicitly defined	Organizational units' exploratory innovation	Heterogeneity in top managers' regulatory foci and coordination mechanisms	Theoretical and empirical
Halberg (2017)	Defined by quoting Abell et al. (2008)	Firm's pricing strategy	Role of individual judgement, human capital, and commercial experience	Theoretical and empirical drawing on a case study

resources, and so on. Yet, as Table 1 illustrates, the set of topics and phenomena covered in the literature is very broad.

Similarly diverse is the way 'microfoundations' is used. Besides some work invoking the term 'microfoundations', which however remains at a single level (e.g., Lewin, Massini, and Peeters, 2011), extant work largely differs along three dimensions.

First, as Table 1 shows, many authors associate microfoundations with analyses that directly involve individuals (e.g., Bridoux, Coeurderoy, and Durand, 2017; Felin and Hesterly, 2007; Hallberg, 2017; Nickerson and Zenger, 2008; Yao and Chang, 2017); others, in turn, simply use the term in the sense of what Felin et al. (2012) call the 'microfoundations as levels' argument and decompose higher-level constructs into lower-level ones, such as, for example, Kim et al. (2016) in explaining the emergence of inter-organizational networks based on firm-level characteristics or use a team-level as foundation for organizational-level phenomena (e.g., Baer, Dirks, and Nickerson, 2013; Lewin, Massini, and Peeters, 2011; Wilden, Devinney, and Dowling, 2016).

Second, there is substantial heterogeneity in the theories and assumptions used in both, the stream of work directly involving individuals as well as the stream following the 'microfoundations as levels' lens. For example, Felin and Hesterly (2007) build on a rational choice-type model; Pentland et al. (2012) or Baer, Dirks, and Nickerson (2013), in contrast, assume that individuals are highly bounded rational; Helfat and Peteraf (2015) and Bitektine and Haack (2015) emphasize cognitive aspects, notably heuristics that help cope with bounded rationality; Gottschalg and Zollo (2007) or Bridoux, Coeurderoy, and Durand (2017), in turn, focus on motivational aspects, such as the difference between extrinsic and intrinsic motivation. An implication that we elaborate later is that microfoundations is a broad set of heuristics that is entirely consistent with a great deal of existing research in economics, psychology, sociology, and so on.[12]

Third, contributions differ in what type of relations of a microfoundational explanation they focus on. We will elaborate on this in detail later in this Element, so we here just note that some work, for example, focuses on how certain individual-level conditions affect the behaviour of the respective individuals in question (what can be termed a 'micro–micro' relation) and how this behaviour then leads to certain organizational-level outcomes (and hence what is typically called a 'micro–macro' relation). Other work, in turn, includes

---

[12] 'Heuristics' here refers to the positive ('dos') and negative ('don'ts') that scientists apply to problem-solving, that is, more or less explicit instructions regarding how to actually carry out scientific activities (cf. Lakatos, 1970).

organizational-level antecedents to the individual-level conditions in their argumentation (a 'macro–micro' relation); whereas some focus exclusively on the 'micro–macro' relation. Thus, for example, Lindenberg and Foss (2011) examine the conditions under which organizational antecedents (e.g., task structure and rewards) may influence individual-level cognition and motivation such that the beneficial organizational consequences of what they call 'joint production motivation' are realized – and, hence, cover all three types of relations. In contrast, Felin and Hesterly's (2007) provocative argument that organizational capabilities are fundamentally epiphenomena of individual-level heterogeneity is an argument that primarily invokes a micro–macro relation. Similarly, some of the works has more than two layers (e.g., individual, group level, and organizational level), whereas other works zoom in onto two layers only. Extant work also differs in whether relations of a single period in time are studied (e.g., the relations leading to the foundation of a new firm) or whether the relations from multiple phases are considered (such as when both the founding of a new venture as well as its long-term survival are considered) (see Saebi, Foss, and Linder, 2019).

2.3 Microfoundational Currents in Management Thinking

If our understanding of microfoundations so far is that it pursues explanation of collective entities, phenomena, and outcomes in terms of the actions and interactions of lower-level entities, are there any currents in contemporary management research, rather than single articles, that we may deem 'microfoundational'? We think there are, even though these have often not been explicitly positioned as microfoundational.

First, parts of the established body of organization theory is clearly microfoundational. This is particularly the case of Organizational Economics (e.g., agency theory, transaction cost economics (TCE), property rights), which builds from explicit assumptions about individuals and the interaction to collective outcomes, such as the choice of contracting arrangements and the efficiency implications of these (e.g., Hart, 1995; Holmström, 1979; Jensen and Meckling, 1976; Williamson, 1985) or work on how to coordinate production (e.g., Dessein, Galeotti, and Santos, 2016; Dessein and Santos, 2006; Marschak and Radner, 1972). Second, the fields of HRM and strategic HRM often have a microfoundational flavour, as these fields explicitly link individuals (i.e., employees, prospective hires, etc.), HR practices, and firm outcomes (e.g., Wright, Coff, and Moliterno, 2014). Third, the emerging field of strategic human capital theory is yet another example. This approach, which has become influential in strategy, explicitly starts from 'human capital' – that is, the skills, capabilities, experience, and so on – as it is embodied in individual employees, managers, and entrepreneurs and examines the motivations to build, extend, and so on human capital in organizations under different assumptions about incentives, distribution of bargaining power, the complementarity and specificity of the relevant human capital, and so on (e.g., Crook et al., 2011). This approach builds from economics and psychology. A fourth example is behavioural strategy which seeks to leverage cognitive and motivational psychology to understand strategic decision-making, as well as, for example, how different motivators impact employee efforts through different psychological mechanisms (e.g., Bridoux and Stoelhorst, 2014).

These currents clearly differ. Organizational economics is fundamentally applied microeconomics, while behavioural strategy is heavily indebted to psychology research. This illustrates the point we made earlier, namely that microfoundations is not a theory, but a set of heuristics for how to theorize (and, subsequently, do empirical research). These principles do impose constraints on theorizing, but these constraints are so relatively unconstraining that they are consistent with significant variety in how microfoundations are built by management scholars. Yet, some of the seeming lack of consistency in terms of how microfoundations are used disappears if one recognizes that the various studies speak to different parts within a common structure of microfoundational explanations. Therefore, before we discuss in more detail what microfoundational work promises to do for research and business practice and what particular research opportunities we see, let's have a closer look at the structure of microfoundational explanations. Delving deeper into the structure of microfoundational explanations will help us refine our initial sketch and arrive at a clearer understanding of what microfoundations are.

3 The Nature of Microfoundations

3.1 What Do Microfoundational Explanations Look Like?

Microfoundational explanations can take various forms. The simplest manifestation (at least conceptually) involves aggregating from a micro- to a macro-level. Examples of this may be showing which outcome emerges in a principal–agent dyad (e.g., Holmström, 1979); how actions taken by team members lead to team outcomes (Mathieu et al., 2008); or demonstrating the welfare properties of a market economy with price-taking and maximizing individuals and firms (Debreu, 1959). As anyone who is familiar with these examples will know, in practice understanding such aggregation from micro to macro can be highly intricate. Adding more mechanisms and levels produces additional complexity, as does making the time dimension explicit (e.g.,

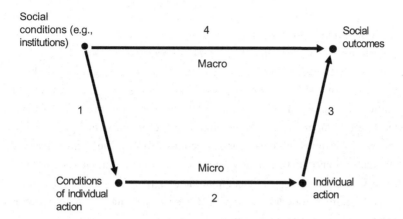

Figure 1 A general model of social science explanation

individuals may learn aggregate outcomes, and their next-period actions are taken in response to such outcomes).

Many phenomena indeed call for such complex approaches, but before we turn to these, gaining an understanding of the basic structure of a microfoundational explanation by looking at a 'simple' one is helpful. The so-called Coleman bathtub or boat, which is depicted in Figure 1, has become the basic workhorse of much of the microfoundations literature, because it provides the essence of microfoundational explanation in perhaps the simplest possible form.

The figure is named after 'rational choice sociologist' James Coleman. In a simple, generic way it depicts the relations of interest in a microfoundational explanation that involves two levels: a macro-level and a micro-level. 'Macro' in this figure may, for example, refer to factors or outcomes on the level of society, an industry, a cartel, a firm, a business unit, or the like. And the figure then tries to visualize what relations help understand why – and in particular, how – certain macro-level outcomes come about. (Those familiar with graph theory will recognize a simple, directed, a-cyclical graph with four nodes and three edges.)

A full microfoundational explanation will typically involve all four nodes and all three Arrows. The phenomenon-to-be-explained, that is, the *explanandum* or *outcome* (or, to use terminology from the statistical variation-based paradigm, the *dependent variable*), is represented by the north-eastern node. The remaining nodes and Arrows are then parts of the *explanans*, or the set of antecedents or independent and mediator variables ('control variables' may be represented as variables that impact on the Arrows from outside the bathtub). The Arrows may be thought of as causal mechanisms that can take different forms. Thus, the Coleman bathtub is a simple example of a multilevel path diagram.

The diagram posits that the north-western node, which contains macro factors (e.g., formal and informal institutions), has a downward causal effect on the predilections and inclinations of individuals (*Arrow 1*). Different institutional set-ups or governance mechanisms or other macro-level factors will differentially impact on lower levels (Kozlowski and Klein, 2000: 14), notably on the conditions faced by individuals. The conditions that an individual is placed in determine the cognition, the motivation, and the opportunities the individual faces, which in turn influences his/her actions (node at the end of *Arrow 2*). Individual actions may then finally form up to social outcomes in different ways (*Arrow 3*), explaining the explanandum phenomenon.

Therefore, microfoundational explanations as characterized by the Coleman diagram, and thus, microfoundations,

- imply a *layered social ontology*, that is, there is an underlying claim that levels exist in social reality. Thus, institutions not only exist, but exist at a level that is supra-individual. (A further implication, to be discussed later, is that bathtubs can be 'stacked').
- involve both *intra- and inter-level causation*. Thus, the relations between the nodes are causal ones (rather than merely constitutive), and the diagram involves upward as well as downward causality
- appeal to *mechanistic explanation*, that is, the Arrows involve parts that interact in a regular, law-like manner (Elster, 1989; Machamer, Darden, and Craver, 2000)
- involve *time*. Thus, the nodes may be thought of time t1, t2, t3, and t4, the Arrows being processes that link these points in time. Thus, the diagram can be seen as a time-dimensioned path diagram (Abell and Engel, 2018)
- stress the *primacy of micro* in the sense that all explanation must always involve reference to micro (whereas the opposite is not always the case). In practice, this accounts for the frequent association of microfoundations with methodological individualism)
- highlight the role of *behaviours and interactions*, that is, things happen because people or groups of people act, given their constraints
- explicitly allow that *collectives* have a role in the explanation, that is, in contrast to popular perception microfoundations do not eliminate macro-level factors from the explanation, as these are placed at the north-western node.

Traditionally, many explanations for phenomena in management (e.g., firm performance; failure of a firm; innovativeness of an organization) have proceeded by what in Coleman's figure is denoted as *Arrow 4*, that is: a macro–macro explanation. An example may be that a firm's strategy, structure, HR policies, IT or control systems cause its performance. As the figure illustrates, such a relation, however, is only kind of a summary of what is going on when considering multiple levels of analysis.

In a perspective considering both the macro- and the micro-levels and how they relate, the relation seemingly portrayed by *Arrow 4* can be decomposed into three Arrows: a macro–micro relation (*Arrow 1*), a micro–micro relation (*Arrow 2*), and a micro–macro one (*Arrow 3*). That is: for example, the strategy–performance relation could be decomposed in how a certain strategy shapes the conditions of individual decision makers in a firm, such as, for example, sales managers (*Arrow 1*), how these individual-level conditions affect the behaviour and interactions of the decision makers (*Arrow 2*), and how these behaviours and interactions translates into firm performance (*Arrow 3*). Hedström and Swedberg (1996: 296–8) refer to *Arrows 1, 2,* and *3* as representing 'situational', 'individual action', and 'transformational' mechanisms, respectively. Taken together, *Arrows 1–3* explain why and how a macro-level variable, like a firm's strategy, leads to a macro-level outcome of interest (here: performance). This explanation runs over two analytical levels (micro and macro) and from left to right.

Research following a microfoundations perspective, however, does not necessarily have to go all that way, that is, cover all of *Arrows 1–3*. As indicated, it may focus on shedding light on how macro outcomes (collective phenomena) result from micro actions and their outcomes (micro phenomena) (Kozlowski and Klein, 2000). For example, the microeconomics of competitive markets analyses situations where market-level outcomes happen when all consumers and firms in a market take prices as given (Debreu, 1959). Conversely, industrial organization economics (Tirole, 1988) studies how outcomes are driven by strategic interaction. Whereas such analyses take certain institutional set-ups for granted, these may be 'suppressed' so that the focus can be concentrated on how individual/firm actions drive collective outcomes. Explanations focusing exclusively on *Arrow 3* thus fall just as much under the term microfoundations as do explanations that *additionally* include *Arrow 2* or, include also both, *Arrows 2* and *1*. In contrast, explanations that precede only in terms of *Arrow 4* (and are not meant only as a shorthand for a known explanation via *1, 2,* and *3*) or that focus exclusively on the micro-level (i.e., only on *Arrow 2*) are not microfoundational. The prior one is not, since (if the explanation isn't only a shorthand for a known microfoundational explanation) it would imply an appeal to macro causality. An appeal to macro causality can, by definition, not be microfoundational as it only involves a single level of analysis, namely the macro-level.

However, what about the macro-level antecedents themselves that we relate in a microfoundational explanation to the macro-level outcomes *via Arrows 1,*

2, and *3*? We stated earlier that microfoundations is entirely consistent with the presence of such macro-level factors in the explanatory apparatus. However, does a microfoundational perspective require assuming them 'as given'? To stay in our example: is firm strategy itself necessarily 'a given' and firm performance the end of a microfoundational explanation? The answer to these questions, 'no'. Microfoundational explanations can well extend to multiperiod analyses, where firm strategy is the macro-level outcome of phase 1 and a macro-level antecedent of some phenomenon (like firm performance) in phase 2 and where both of these phases involve explanations of the macro–micro, micro–micro, and micro–macro types (e.g., Linder and Foss, 2018). In fact, while microfoundational explanation allows for the presence of aggregates or collectives in the explanation, ultimately such macro-level factors should be shown to result from individuals and their interactions. We will look into these explanations as well as into explanations with more than two levels in the following section.

3.2 Complex Microfoundations: Extending the Coleman Bathtub

The 'Coleman bathtub' as depicted in Figure 1 is a directed graph, where some antecedents on the left of the diagram cause via some micro- and cross-level mechanisms the outcomes on the right side of the figure. This implies that it is implicitly time-dimensioned, such that *Arrow 1* occurs before *Arrow 2* which occurs before *Arrow 3*. And, in fact, a microfoundational analysis also allows for the macro-level facts/institutions in the upper-left node to be themselves explained in a microfoundational way. Such a multistage explanation corresponds to adding a Coleman diagram to the left of the focal diagram.

Figure 2 provides an example for such a two-stage diagram. Consider, for example, organizational goals. In management research, these can be taken as either the explanans or the explanandum – or both (Linder and Foss, 2018). For example, researchers may be interested in how organizational goals form and why firms in the same industry may have different goals (i.e., goals as an explanandum), or they might focus on the effects of different organizational goals for organizational-level outcomes (i.e., goals as part of the explanans). Or, they may be interested in studying both 'stages', that is, what shapes organizational goals and their adoption, and how such goals in turn have consequences, possibly leading to goal revision in a third stage.

Like organizational goals, many phenomena of interest to management scholars and practitioners merit microfoundational analyses stretching multiple phases. In practice, this often translates into different research projects, each

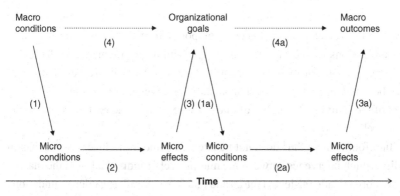

(1)/(1a) Bridge assumptions   (2)/(2a)Micro-level behavioural theory   (3)/(3a) Transformation rules

Figure 2 Time in microfoundational explanation – example: organizational goals

focusing on the microfoundations of a particular stage. For example, strategy researchers are certainly interested in better understanding how a particular firm strategy leads to certain performance outcome (i.e., strategy content research-ers). However, they may also wonder what brought about that strategy or how certain performance outcomes affect subsequent strategy-formation processes (i.e., strategy process research). HRM researchers may, for example, be inter-ested not only in the effects of certain high-performance work practices for the extant workforce, but also why and how firms exhibiting these practices arrived at using them. Similarly, researchers and practitioners in organization or orga-nizational control may want to better understand both the effects of certain structural arrangements or control tools, and what let these organizations to exhibit these arrangements or use the tools. All of these – and many more such questions – are amenable to microfoundational analysis.

It is clear that for many of these questions, placing relevant factors, variables, and phenomena into two levels (micro and macro) only is a rather coarse representation of reality. For example, if we think of 'macro' as the firm level and 'micro' as the level of individuals, where are groups, teams, units, depart-ments, divisions, and so on? This may prompt introduction of a 'meso'-level. For example, firm strategy or organizational goals are likely decided by a team of top managers – and, hence, an entity that in some sense neither operates on (nor is placed at) the individual nor the firm level.

Recall, however, that the microfoundations approach (in its microfounda-tions as a levels argument version) is flexible with respect to what is 'micro' and what is 'macro'. Thus, an analysis studying how a team of top managers decides upon a strategy for their organization by focusing on the conditions of the individual members of the TMT and how they affect their actions and how these, in turn, affect the group's decision is just as much compatible with the idea of microfoundations as it is to decompose a firm's strategy or performance into the actions of the various subgroups within an organization (the TMT, division heads, department heads, 'ordinary employees', the representatives of the labour union, etc.). Moreover, analyses may cover all three levels, that is, the level of the individual member of one of these groups, the group level, and the firm level.

Microfoundations thus does not negate that some meso-level often exists in reality, which intervenes between the micro-level of individuals and the macro-level of organizational-level factors and outcomes. Similarly, microfoundations allows for expansions of the macro – such as differentiating the macro into, for example, the level of a single firm, the level of strategic groups, an industry, the economy, or society as a whole. In the Coleman diagram, adding a meso-level or differentiating the macro-level further leads to 'stacked' bathtubs, as illustrated in Figure 3 for the case of organizational goals.

An Example: Corporate Social Responsibility and Organizational Goals

Figure 3 offers a simplified visualization of some of the elements of an explanation of how organizational goals (i.e., a firm-level construct) are affected by the mounting society-level pressure from numerous sides, including, but not limited to, the media, customers, governments, and activists, for what may be broadly described as 'corporate social responsibility' (CSR) (Garriga and Melé, 2004; McWilliams and Siegel, 2001).[13] CSR can be linked to three phenomena (Foss and Linder, 2019: (1) a rejection of shareholders taking primacy over other stakeholders in value creation and distribution (e.g., Donaldson and Preston, 1995; Freeman, 1994; Freeman, Wicks, and Parmar, 2004); (2) a pressure that organizations satisfy the needs of a their stakeholders today 'without compromising the ability to meet the needs of future stakeholders' (Dyllick and Hockerts, 2002: 131); and (3) a growing expectation (and in some cases legal requirement) that organizations disclose their performance on multiple 'bottom lines', that is, the performance with respect to satisfying the needs of their various stakeholders, so to create transparency and thereby force organizations to better satisfy the needs of all stakeholders (Cho et al., 2015; Norman and MacDonald, 2004).

---

[13] The term 'corporate social responsibility' is used in many different ways and has evolved considerably over the years (e.g., Carroll, 1999; Garriga and Melé, 2004; Matten and Moon, 2008; Perera Aldama and Zicari, 2012). For pragmatic reasons, we use it here as an umbrella term to discuss a set of efforts by firms to conduct business in a manner that reflects the social and environmental imperatives and consequences of business success (Barnett, 2007; Matten and Moon, 2008).

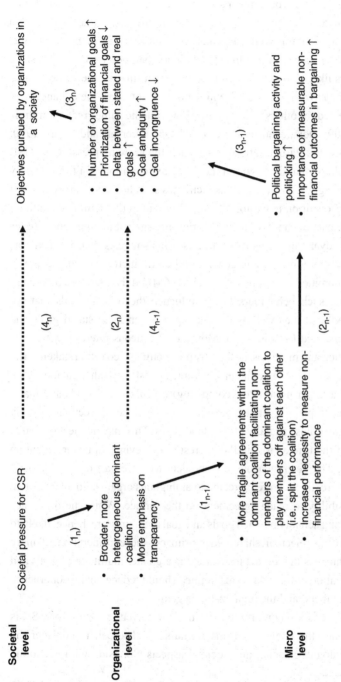

Figure 3 Cross- and micro-effects of the pressure for corporate social responsibility on organizational goal formation

The growing pressure for CSR implies a broadening of the population of stakeholders who can become part of the firm's dominant coalition. Stakeholders who before had difficulty justifying themselves having a say in the firm's decision-making need to be taken more into account in the deals done, favours, and debts traded among the stakeholders than before. However, since all stakeholders likely have their own preferences, furthering the value created for one stakeholder (or group of stakeholders) may not allow the enhancement of the value created for others or even imply lowering the value created for these (Devinney, 2009; Donaldson and Preston, 1995; Freeman and Evan, 1990; Freeman, Wicks, and Parmar, 2004). Therefore, the growing pressure for CSR raises the likelihood that deals within the dominant coalition of a firm are only temporary and fragile (*Arrow 1 $_n$*). This facilitates stakeholders who are not part of the dominant coalition to exploit this fragility within the dominant coalition by playing one part of the dominant coalition off against another one (*Arrow 1 $_{n-1}$*), thereby advancing their own interests. This suggests that political bargaining activity and politicking in general in the firm increase (*Arrow 2 $_{n-1}$*).

As already submitted by Cyert and March (1963) and the literature on organizational politics, such behaviours likely influence the official goals that the organization formulates as well as the overlap between these stated goals and the real goals pursued (*Arrow 3 $_{n-1}$*). More heterogeneous interests within the dominant coalition and more possibilities by non-dominant coalition stakeholders to play off groups within the dominant coalition against each other entail that the firm settles for a larger number of (competing) organizational goals and that – given a likely incompatibility in these goals – the difference between the publicly espoused goals and those actually pursued increases. This may not be apparent to the members of the firm as it is in the interest of achieving some agreement on common goals. The heterogeneous stakeholders who are part of the dominant coalition, therefore, likely prefer agreeing to ambiguous organizational goals that afford the possibility to reach agreement on the surface. While the difference between stated and actually pursued goals and goal ambiguity are, hence, likely to increase due to the reject of shareholder primacy, the consideration of more stakeholders' interests in the goal formation via a greater multitude of goals and a lower prioritization of financial goals implied should reduce goal incongruence between the members' and the organization's goals.

Moreover, there is a second route by which the current pressure for CSR is likely to influence the goals that firms formulate.[14] The call to consider the longer-term ecological, social, and societal aspects alongside with economic

---

[14] It may well be that there are other routes in addition to the two considered here, such as the incomplete contracting approach in Asher, Mahoney, and Mahoney (2005). Since our objective in this section is not to lay out a full-blown theory of CSR, but simply to illustrate how

ones in doing business, thereby ensuring the long-term viability (along these three dimensions) of meeting the needs of the stakeholders (e.g., Cho et al., 2015; Dyllick and Hockerts, 2002), requires firms to be transparent about the long(er)-term consequences of today's actions (*Arrow 1* $_n$). Non-financial indicators are commonly seen to be more forward-looking than financial ones (Kaplan and Norton, 1992). Thus, CSR implies a need to complement financial information with more non-financial one than was necessary before. Such information needs to be generated. Managers and employees within firms thus need to devise systems and measures for capturing the non-financial consequences of their (firm's) actions. These efforts not only draw more attention to the non-financial consequences of one's actions – thereby likely rendering them more present in internal discussions and bargaining in decision-making – but are also costly in terms of time. Since time is a scarce resource, many organizational members likely prefer suggesting easy-to-measure non-financial outcomes, while difficult-to-measure outcomes may be sidelined (*Arrow 2* $_{n-1}$). Besides this unintentional bias, some members of the organization may also deliberately advance some measures as they deem them helpful for advancing their own interests within internal bargaining processes (*Arrow 2* $_{n-1}$). Both the deliberate as well as the non-deliberate bias introduced are likely to affect the content and nature of the goals that the firm adopts (*Arrow 3* $_{n-1}$). Thus, it likely influences the content and prioritization among the organizational goals, as the metrics available during the political bargaining processes within the goal formulation have been suggested to serve as non-neutral language (Burchell et al., 1980). The increased importance of easily measurable non-financial outcomes in the bargaining makes it tempting to assume that CSR reduces goal ambiguity as measurable outcomes allow setting rather precise targets (e.g., 'reduce CO_2 emissions by 3 per cent each year'). The overall impact, however, will depend on the relative strength of the effect from reporting versus the competing effect of the reject of shareholder primacy discussed earlier.

As this example illustrates, microfoundational explanations are neither limited to only two levels, nor to a single phase in time. Microfoundations are, in fact, quite flexible with respect to what and how many levels or what phase(s) one is interested in. However, it is true that analyses spanning more than two levels or multiple periods quickly get fairly complex to visualize as well as to analyse. Obviously, this effect is even stronger for analyses that extend the basic 'bathtub', both in the time (horizontal) as well as the levels (vertical) dimensions. While it may be tempting to go for 'comprehensive'

---

a microfoundational argumentation looks like, we concentrate here on only two of the conceivable avenues.

models, it thus may often be more pragmatic to focus on shedding light at the various sub-models of such a comprehensive model first before trying to put all things together. We will return to this point later when we discuss what we consider to be particularly fruitful avenues for microfoundational research.

4 Critiques of Microfoundations

The growing microfoundations movement is not greeted with universal enthusiasm by all. Critical reactions have ranged from claims that microfoundations are trivial and noncontroversial,[15] over arguments that microfoundations is merely a relabelling exercise for smuggling psychology ideas into strategy to claims that microfoundations research is empirically 'too difficult' (we have heard them all!). Barney and Felin (2013) offer a useful survey and discussion of the critique of microfoundations, which Felin, Foss, and Ployhart (2015) extend. Felin and Spender (2009) have an interesting debate between a proponent of microfoundations and a more sceptical scholar.

In the following we draw on these discussions and add to them in the light of recently voiced criticism (e.g., Epstein, 2015). Some critiques are indeed fundamental, such as those concerning the value added of microfoundations, and, the novelty or difference of microfoundations from other, extant research streams (e.g., OB, strategic HRM, multilevel research). Other points relate to specific aspects of microfoundations, such as claims or arguments concerning specific microfoundational assumptions (e.g., that there is no macro–macro causality). We first look at the points related to the value-added of microfoundations; subsequently, we turn to the points about assumptions.

4.1 What is the Value Added of Microfoundations?[16]

It is often claimed that management theory and practice are characterized by fads and fashions where old insights are rediscovered and questionably rebranded, become a fad, and then fade, only to be rediscovered later. We doubt this is descriptively entirely correct, but it is undeniable that there often seems to be some kind of herd behaviour and it is thus quite natural that many scholars (and practitioners!) have acquired a certain cautionary attitude towards new or seemingly new practices and tools and apply high thresholds for separating true intellectual innovation from mere relabelled ideas. Consequently, before 'jumping on the bandwagon' many scholars will carefully look at how a newly proposed

---

[15] The paper that Winter (2013) identified as the 'opening salvo' in the microfoundations debate in management research, namely Felin and Foss (2005) was rejected by a leading ('A+') management journal with exactly the claim that microfoundations were non-controversial in strategy research. Subsequent debate has revealed that this is very far from the truth.

[16] This draws on Felin, Foss, and Ployhart (2015).

approach or perspective differs from what already exists and what additional value the new one offers above and beyond what is already being offered.

This is also the case for microfoundations. Indeed, in the eyes of at least some sceptical scholars, microfoundations seems to fail the test of value added in the value that microfoundations offers above and beyond what (Strategic) HRM (SHRM), I/O Psychology, OB, and multilevel research already offer.

Individuals form the starting point in the 'microfoundations as explanatory primacy of individuals' view. Not surprisingly, some wonder how microfoundations links with, is similar or different to, micro disciplines such as OB, industrial and organizational psychology (I/O psychology), and HR. After all, the focus of OB, I/O psychology, and HR is on individuals (e.g., individual differences in ability, motivation, and personality), interactions (e.g., small groups and teams), mechanisms (e.g., task and process characteristics), and context (e.g., organizational climate, leadership). Some have thus suggested that microfoundations is simply a relabelling exercise or is simply about borrowing concepts from other disciplines and fields. Similarly, some have questioned as to whether microfoundations is just a relabelling of multilevel research.

Microfoundations are by definition (and irrespective of which one of the two views of microfoundations one follows) concerned with *at least* two levels. Thus, it seems tempting to simply equate microfoundations with multilevel research. We readily acknowledge that there are similarities between microfoundations and both the micro literatures and multilevel research. However, as we explain below in more detail, simply equating microfoundations with micro disciplines or multilevel research is based on an erroneous understanding of what microfoundations are.

Microfoundations versus Micro Disciplines

As we explained when discussing the explanatory structure of microfoundations in terms of the Coleman bathtub (Figure 1), explanations that precede only in terms of *Arrow 2* and that therefore focus exclusively on the micro-level are not microfoundational. They involve only a single level of analysis: the micro-level. However, microfoundations, imply that something is the foundation of something else. Hence, an explanation including *Arrow 2* should be accompanied at least by *Arrow 3* to qualify as microfoundational. The focus of the above micro literatures is, however, primarily on *Arrow 2*. As Felin, Foss, and Ployhart (2015) and Ployhart and Hendricks (2019) argue, it is rare for the micro literatures to consider *Arrow 3* if the social outcome is operationalized at the firm level or higher and within a macro context. Thus, the most common outcomes studied within the micro literature are individual outcomes, such as job performance and satisfaction, as well as small group outcomes, but not firm-level outcomes. Interestingly, while *Arrow 3* is neglected in such research, this is also somewhat the case of *Arrow 1*. As we argued earlier, microfoundations are entirely consistent with contextual factors playing an explanatory role. However, scholars have often questioned the extent to which context plays a meaningful role in OB (Rousseau and Fried, 2001; Johns, 2006). Paradoxically, despite the term 'organization' in OB, there is little *explicit* attention paid to incorporating the organizational context (Whetten, Felin, and King, 2009) (see further, Felin et al., 2015), which is taken to be a sort of anonymous background variable. In contrast, a microfoundations focus moves the macro context from background to foreground. Microfoundations, therefore, pushes micro research towards a broader focus, because it highlights that individuals are placed in a particular macro context. Thus, as Felin, Foss and Ployhart (2015) note, microfoundations might be seen as fundamentally concerned with what Heath and Sitkin (2001) label big-O (Ob) rather than big-B (oB)-type of organizational research. Heath and Sitkin highlight how scholarship in OB tends to be of the latter variety, where the research is only incidentally about organizations and more so about behaviour. Thus, microfoundations does offer value added above and beyond what the micro disciplines already offer.

Microfoundations versus Multilevel Research

Like multilevel research, microfoundations subscribes to a layered social ontology, that is, there is an underlying claim that levels are not just analytical categories but may exist in social reality. Yet, besides this common point, microfoundations, irrespective of whether one follows the 'primacy of individuals' or the 'as a levels' view, differs significantly from the kind of multilevel research and modelling that many scholars in recent years have called for (e.g., Aguinis et al., 2011; Hitt et al., 2007; Mathieu and Chen, 2011).[17]

As outlined earlier when we discussed the nature of microfoundational explanations and when presenting the Coleman diagram, microfoundations seeks to advance our understanding of phenomena by locating (theoretically and empirically) the proximate causes of a phenomenon (or explanations of an outcome) at one or more levels of analysis lower than that of the phenomenon

---

[17] However, recently some attempts in multilevel research at accounting for microfoundational perspectives are visible – for example, in some contributions to the newly published *Handbook of Multilevel Theory, Measurement, and Analysis* edited by Stephen Humphrey and James LeBreton.

itself. The underlying belief is that knowledge and science can be advanced by means of reductive operations (Felin et al., 2012).

In contrast, the multilevel approach is largely theoretically agnostic about which level of analysis, a priori, may have the most significant impact in the analysis (Felin, Foss, and Ployhart, 2015).[18] Explanations based on concepts located at one or more levels of analysis above that of the phenomenon of interest are thus just as much compatible with the calls for multilevel research as are studies drawing on explanations based on levels of analysis lower than the phenomenon. Thus, even the microfoundations as a levels view differs from the multilevel research approach (as it gives primacy to whatever level is deemed 'micro'). One may claim that microfoundations is a specific form of multilevel research that insists that macro influences are always mediated through micro mechanisms. In sum, microfoundations implies a quest for potential micro explanations of heterogeneous macro outcomes and emphasizes bottom-up influence, aggregation, and different forms of emergence (Felin, Foss, and Ployhart, 2015). For example, arguing that a firm's source of value can be found in its network relationships would lead microfoundations scholars to ask immediate questions about the origins of these relationships or network – the nested, causal antecedents. In contrast, the multilevel approach does not privilege any particular analytical level. Thus, while both start from a layered ontology, the two differ significantly in the nature of their explanations and microfoundations clearly does offer added value over a simple multilevel perspective.

4.2 Assumptions in Microfoundational Explanation

In addition to critique regarding the value added of microfoundations, what are argued to be assumptions of microfoundations has sparked significant critique of the microfoundations movement. Notice our qualifier, 'what are argued to be'! Thus, microfoundations has been said (i) to imply reductionism; (ii) to deny the role of structure and macro factors; (iii) to be an attempt to smuggle in assumptions from neoclassical economics via the 'back door' into management research; (iv) to be merely a 'warmed up' methodological individualism; and (v) to imply an infinite regress (Barney and Felin, 2013; Hodgson, 2012; Winter, 2011). In the following we briefly evaluate these points.

---

[18] Empirically, as Felin et al. (2015) lay out in more detail, early multilevel research (e.g., Lieberson and O'Connor, 1972; McGahan and Porter, 1997; Rumelt, 1991; Schmalensee, 1985) has contended itself with theory-independent or neutral efforts to see which level of analysis mattered most for performance (e.g., industry, corporate, business, leadership).

Microfoundations as Reductionism

A common critique of microfoundations is that it implies 'reductionism'. Typically, reductionism is seen as an explanatory position submitting that the best understanding of a complex collective-level phenomenon 'should be sought at the level of structure, behaviour and laws of its component parts plus their relations' (Silberstein, 2002: 81). Such reductionism may in turn be seen as part of a broader mechanism-based approach to explanation, one that addresses the 'cogs and wheels' (Elster 1989: 3) that generate and explain observed associations between events (Machamer, Darden, and Craver, 2000; cf. Hedström and Swedberg, 1996). In this view, causality means accounting for how a set of interacting entities that carry out interrelated or interactional activities produce the social and collective phenomenon of interest.[19] Many, and perhaps most, theorists of science today would probably agree that producing such accounts is the essence of science and that increasing the 'grain' or level of detail of such accounts is a very frequent instance of scientific progress (Elster, 1989). Foss (2012) provides an account of the progressive evolution of strategic management thinking in terms of a quest towards digging deeper and deeper in the explanation of competitive advantage, descending the hierarchy of levels of analysis from the industry to individual resources and their characteristics.

Reductive operations may increase explanatory complexity. Moving from single-level explanation to explanation involving more than one analytical level almost inherently increases such complexity. Additionally, complexity is increased because microfoundational explanation seeks to account for how mechanisms unfold *over time*. As Lewis (1986: 214) explains, '[a]ny particular event that we might wish to explain stands at the end of a long and complicated causal history. We might imagine a world where causal histories are short and simple; but in the world as we know it, the only question is whether they are infinite or merely enormous.' Thus, empirically, a microfoundational explanation may seem to quickly explode in complexity as each and every action and interaction that may have a bearing on the phenomenon under investigation need to be accounted for. However, explanatory parsimony is also important, but may seem to run counter to microfoundational explanation.

---

[19] More broadly, a 'mechanism ... is a set of entities and activities organized such they exhibit the phenomenon to be explained' (Craver, 2007: 5). Explanation that proceeds in terms of accounting for such generative mechanisms differs from the traditional covering-law model of explanation, because the covering-law model does not imply a commitment to identifying causal mechanisms and their operation, but instead stresses explanation as subsuming an event under general laws – which, however, is often 'explanation' with unobserved mechanisms.

Luckily, it is not always necessary to perform 'rock-bottom explanations' or to refer only to individual-level facts for a microfoundational explanation to be valid. As we have already explained (Section 3), collectives and aggregate context can be admitted into such explanation. Additionally, often explanation can proceed by focusing on 'average' or 'representative' actors (as in the 'representative agent' explanation in economics). Also, it may sometimes be acceptable to suppress an account of micro mechanisms in the interest of explanatory parsimony. For example, basic economics suggests that, under competitive conditions, decision makers in firms only have a limited feasible behavioural repertoire, as many actions are not consistent with long-run survival and therefore will not be considered. Thus, context dictates certain behaviours, and context (here, competitive conditions) may therefore substitute in an explanatory sense for a much more complicated explanation involving individual action and interaction (Satz and Ferejohn, 1994).

In sum, while microfoundational explanation can be seen as an example of a general scientific quest for reduction, there are also (pragmatic) limits to such reduction. When we discuss empirical research strategies later in this Element, we will discuss other such pragmatic limits.

Microfoundations as Denying the Role of Structure and Macro Factors

As we have stressed throughout, the primary goal of the microfoundations programme of research is to unpack macro concepts and to identify the micro-level mechanisms that mediate between macro determinants and macro outcomes. This already suggests that microfoundations do not imply a denial of the relevance of macro constructs in explanation, a point we also made in connection with our discussion in Section 3 of the Coleman diagram.

While much of the emphasis of microfoundational research is on aggregation and emergence, the contextual (macro) factors of an organization also play a central role. Obvious contextual factors, for example, are organizational structure, production processes, IT and control systems, or incentives. For example, Foss (2003) highlights how the shift from a hierarchical structure to a flatter, more market-based structure at Oticon led to increased innovation and substantially different composite and organizational outcomes. His narrative traces how this change in organization design influenced the motivation and opportunities of organizational members, and links these to firm-level innovation outcomes. Likewise, tacit and explicit forms of knowledge exist at the individual and collective levels and that together influence outcomes (Spender, 1996). Martinkenaite and Breunig (2016) offer a microfoundations analysis that picks up on this insight and explains firm-level absorptive capacity based on sequentially linked learning processes where individual and organizational-level knowledge and abilities interact. Another contribution of the microfoundations movement has been to examine the role that disparate organizational forms or governance structures play in knowledge and information aggregation (Felin and Zenger, 2011).

Very substantial research opportunities remain in further theorizing and empirically examining these linkages. Much of this has to do with the traditional divide between (macro) organizational theory and (micro) OB, which has had the unfortunate consequences of leaving many macro–micro and micro–macro mechanisms ill-understood. Even theories, such as TCE (Williamson, 1985, 1996), that purport to examine such links only examine a small subset of the meaningful links. For example, Foss and Weber (2016) criticize the way that bounded rationality is conceptualized in TCE (namely, as agents being 'intendedly rational but only limitedly so' (Simon, 1961, xxiv)). However, research on bounded rationality adds much more specificity and content to this behavioural assumption. In other words, the microfoundations of TCE are very 'thin'. Building on rich models of bounded rationality, Foss and Weber show that different hierarchical forms (i.e., unitary, multidivisional, and matrix forms) have a very different impact on the bounded rationality of organizational members and therefore give rise to different transaction costs. In a later paper Foss, Lindenberg, and Weber (2019) also examine how different hierarchical forms impact opportunism differentially.

Microfoundations as Methodological Individualism

Historically much of the work on microfoundations has been aligned with methodological individualism, that is, the position that all macro social phenomena be reduced to the actions of individuals (as well as with ontological individualism, i.e., the position that only individuals are capable of action, collectives are not). Therefore, one is quickly tempted to see microfoundations as little more than methodological individualism in a new dress and to generalize all critique voiced against methodological individualism and work on building individualistic assumptions to the microfoundations view. Rejecting the microfoundations view for this reason may seem particularly compelling, given the recent debate about social sciences suffering from being stuck in an 'ant trap' due to much of it building on individualistic foundations (Epstein, 2015). Yet, the claim that progress in social sciences been hampered by it building on individualistic foundations and a false analogy between social and natural sciences has so far remained an unsupported assertion (Sugden, 2016: 1378). Moreover, much of the critique of microfoundations as methodological individualism seems to overlook that there are not only multiple types of microfoundations, but equally of methodological individualism.

First, in what we called 'microfoundations as a levels' argument, microfoundations are about reductive operations that make entities and phenomena explainable in terms of what goes on at a lower level. That level may or may not (e.g., Kim et al., 2016) be that of individuals and their interaction. Thus, microfoundations do not necessarily(!) involve methodological individualism. In fact, methodological individualism can rather be seen as a narrower kind of microfoundations. That being said, ultimately, however, it is only individuals that act (even if sometimes on behalf of a group or some 'entity'). So, although one may for methodological reasons assume that, for example, groups or firms act, ultimately understanding those group and firm actions can be advanced by studying individual conditions and interactions of individuals.

Second, methodological individualism comes in different forms (Hodgson, 2012). In the most extreme version of methodological individualism there is no meaningful role for macro constructs in explanation. As should be clear, we do not endorse this version of methodological individualism. The Coleman bathtub model that we have been using throughout rules it out (as it allows for a top-down influence from macro to micro). More generally, we subscribe to what Agassi (1960) calls 'institutional individualism' which recognizes that institutions and other macro structures exist and influence individual choices. Obviously, this position does not rule out that those structures themselves can be explained in terms of individual actions and interactions.

Microfoundations as Infusing Management with Traditional Neoclassical Economics

An initial, critical reaction was that microfoundations was about infusing (strategic) management with traditional neoclassical economics (Winter, 2011), as 'the idea that explanations that are based on individual-level assumptions are superior to, or more satisfying than, those that are not is deeply rooted in the practice of economics' (Sugden, 2016: 1379). However, so far the only microfoundations contribution that perhaps might be seen as 'neoclassical' is Abell, Felin, and Foss (2008), while, for example, contributions such as Gavetti (2005), Gottschalg and Zollo (2007), and Teece (2007) base their microfoundational theorizing on ideas that are very different from – and even at variance with – this branch of economics.

In contrast to the ill-footed claim that microfoundations are simply introducing traditional economics via the backdoor, one might therefore question whether microfoundations are maybe too 'underdetermined' as they virtually

allow for any model of human rationality and behaviour to form the foundation –
including the 'zero intelligence traders' of some extreme finance models
(Sunder and Gode, 1993), the various models of bounded rationality (Simon,
1955), and even the extreme rationality of game theory (cf. Stirling and Felin,
2013). In fact, a central part of the debate has concerned the forms of rationality
that are allowed into our analysis (Felin and Foss, 2012; Hodgson and Knudsen,
2011; Winter, 2011). In sum, microfoundations are *not* about smuggling neoclassical economics into management research.

Microfoundations Imply an Infinite Regress

Since microfoundations calls for developing explanations of higher-level phenomena by departing from lower-level phenomena or actors as the proximate
causes; it is not surprising that some scholars have raised the issue of what exactly
this lower level should be. Relatedly, the argument has been made whether a call
for microfoundations does not simply imply an infinite regress of micro-level
explanations by even more micro-level ones. Thus, if one takes microfoundations
seriously, why would an explanation of, say, firm performance *via* the behaviours
of the firm's CEO be satisfactory? Wouldn't a full explanation involve explaining
these behaviours by even more micro-level factors, such as the genes of the
individual – or perhaps even parentage, ancestry, and so on? Given the nested
nature of institutions (Friedland and Alford, 1991), where 'everything is micro to
something and macro to something else' (Harmon, Haack, and Roulet, 2019:
465), such a question is more than legitimate.

However, while the question is legitimate, there are several answers to it –
and, hence, dismissing the microfoundations lens based on it – as some
scholars do – is misguided. First, it is usually entirely legitimate in scientific
explanations to black box very distant causes (see Barney and Felin, 2013),
irrespective of whether they are at the macro- or the micro-level. Second, the
worry that microfoundations lead to an infinite regress relates to a familiar
problem (and source of debate) for macro organizational scholars: the temporal interdependence between structure and agency (agency is influenced by
structure, which is explainable in terms of actions that are influenced by
structure) (cf. Winter, 2012b; Cardinale, 2018). In fact, even some form of
'macrofoundations' could be said to suffer from the same 'infinite regress'
issue since '[e]ach level of an organizational system is embedded or included
in a higher-level context' (Kozlowski and Klein, 2000: 14). Thus, if industry
structure (macro) determines firms' conduct and, ultimately, performance,
then likely technology and global trade conditions determine (at least in
part) industry structure as macro factors. Yet, technology and global trade

conditions, in turn, again could be viewed as being driven by macro factors, such as the stock of human knowledge on this planet or history in a 'macrofoundations' view. Hence, the 'issue' of regress is by no means one specific to microfoundations. Third, and most importantly, it is possible to 'escape' such regress by looking at 'natural stopping' points (Coleman, 1990) for microfoundations in the social sciences.

Felin, Foss, and Ployhart (2015) offer some guidance on what these stopping points may be in management and organization research. Notably, they point to such punctuating events as the founding of a firm. Founders make consequential decisions that leave a lasting imprint on organizations and their trajectory and even performance (Johnson, 2007; Stinchcombe, 1965). Thus, the infinite regress problem can be 'solved' in the sense that there are natural initial conditions, punctuations, and starting points for social analysis, the individual (and associated decision-making) providing a particularly salient one. That said, the critique of infinite regress is understandable and one that in fact haunts any discipline or analysis. The strong form argument for microfoundations indeed might be seen as being particularly susceptible to the infinite regress critique, where explanations of any social phenomena ought to be reduced to 'rock bottom' foundations and the psychological states of individuals (Udehn, 2002).

5 Empirical Microfoundations Research[20]

5.1 Data for Microfoundations Research

Data Source and Measurement Levels

In Section 2 we documented the increase in microfoundational research over the last decade. This includes a growing number of *empirical* microfoundations papers, mainly emerging over the last five to seven years. Perhaps because unfolding the empirical side of microfoundations is rather recent, there has so far been little discussion of the empirical challenges of microfoundations (but see Aguinis and Molina-Azorin, 2015). However, this is an issue that cannot be neglected. Management research is a fundamentally empirical enterprise, and an approach or a theory cannot in the longer run become successful if it is not empirically supported. If microfoundations cannot demonstrate that it adds something also in the empirical dimension, then the current microfoundations enthusiasm will peter out.

---

[20] This subsection partly draws on Abell, Foss, and Lyngsie (Empirical microfoundations for management research. Unpublished working paper, Copenhagen: Department of Strategic Management and Globalization, Copenhagen Business School).

Empirical microfoundations research poses a number of challenges above and beyond those that management scholars encounter in (most) other empirical work. The reason lies in the basic feature of microfoundational thinking: the emphasis it places on enhancing our understanding of macro-level phenomena by means of micro-level explanation, such that it by definition spans at least two levels of analysis.

A key challenge for empirical microfoundations research, therefore, is to identify the right source of empirical data. This may seem like a platitude as it may seem to apply to any research and most PhD courses these days discuss the pros and cons of various data sources, notably primary and secondary data. Yet, here the challenge is less related to questions of primary (e.g., doing one's own new survey or running a series of interviews with decision makers) versus secondary data (data from an extant database, such as Bankscope, CapitalIQ, or the like), but rather to the question of how the constructs situated on a higher analytical level than the individual level should best be captured.

For many years, a significant amount of large sample empirical research in management relied on one key informant per organization, such as the firm's CEO, CFO, head of sales, HR manager, and so on. However, increasingly survey-based research relies on multiple respondents per organization (e.g., Foss and Lyngsie, 2017). Reliance on multiple respondents per organization has been promoted primarily for reducing the risk of common method bias, that is, the systematic error variance shared among variables that are based on the basis of using the same data source (or method) (e.g., Podsakoff et al., 2003). Research on proper research methods (notably multi-trait-multi-method research) suggests that capturing constructs that are situated on a level higher than the individual – such as, organizational capability or organizational culture – by means of multiple informants per organization is preferable to single informant designs. This is not only a matter of minimizing common method bias, but also because informants may disagree, perhaps substantially, about the prevailing condition of such a higher-order construct. Individuals differ in their perceptions and, therefore, may exhibit significant variation in how they assess some higher-order constructs or phenomena. The size of this disagreement depends on whether these constructs or phenomena are directly and reliably observable (aspects of the formal structure of the organization or the properties of the firm's incentive system) or more matters of perception (as in the case of organizational climate, the leadership style of the CEO). Directly and readily observable constructs lead to less variability in assessment – and thus a single informant can provide sufficiently valid data for them (Kozlowski and Klein, 2000).[21]

---

[21] A single informant may also serve as a data source in case she has unique access to relevant information. Kozlowski and Klein (2000) give the examples of a unit manager providing information on the percentage of men, respectively women in the unit she supervises or unit

In many other cases, however – notably for those where a construct of interest is what can be termed a 'shared property' (Kozlowski and Klein, 2000: 37) – reliance on single informants for assessing such a construct is likely to lead to biased data. Kozlowski and Klein (2000) offer the example of measuring organizational climate, which the literature suggests stems from individuals' interpretations of the situation and is an emergent phenomenon. Consequently, a single informant is unlikely to know the inner interpretations of the setting by multiple people within the organization – and, thus, typically will not be a good source of data for measuring the unit-level construct of climate. Thus, for such shared properties or phenomena that are not isomorphic (that is, 'phenomena that are essentially the same as they emerge upward across levels' (Kozlowski and Klein, 2000: 16)) but rather 'phenomena that comprise a common domain but are distinctively different as they emerge across levels' (Kozlowski and Klein, 2000: 16), multiple respondents are necessary in micro-foundations research.

How to best measure shared properties (e.g., an organization's climate) in large sample studies also has been the subject of some debate in literature on multilevel research, and the insights from that literature apply to micro-foundations, too. Notably, different views exist on the best framing of items for shared properties as individual ('I think my company has an open work climate') or at a higher-level ('We think our company has an open work climate') measure (Kozlowski and Klein, 2000). Moreover, some have advised to use items drawing on descriptions, rather than evaluations (James and Jones, 1974). Yet, as already Kozlowski and Klein (2000: 38) noted, 'more empirical work is needed to establish which item characteristics are critical to construct fidelity and which ones are not essential'. While Kozlowski and Klein's assessment now is almost twenty years old and refers to multilevel research in OB, the situation today with respect to microfoundations research is not that much different.[22] The lack of tested guidelines thus is one of the challenges of doing empirical microfoundations research and for assessing the implications of varying designs for theory building and testing.

---

members' tenure. In these examples, the respondent, while an individual, can be expected to provide reliable information on the unit-level constructs of gender distribution, respectively, tenure.

[22] This is not to negate some notable progress within multilevel research, notably, points published in Jebb et al. (2019) and Krasikova and LeBreton (2019). Yet, as outlined earlier, multilevel and microfoundations research differ. Therefore, some adjustments in the guidelines when transferred to microfoundations research may be necessary. Such an assessment is currently lacking in the literature on microfoundations.

Time Scale

As we argued in Section 3, a natural way to think of the Coleman diagram is as a time-dimensioned directed, a-cyclical graph (Abell and Engel, 2018), If one accepts such a view of microfoundations, time and process are inherently built into microfoundational explanations, and they thus seem difficult to conduct empirically on the basis of cross-sectional data (if at all). Yet, even when scholars opt for lagged cross-sections or longitudinal data, a microfoundations lens implies a particular challenge, well-known to scholars in multilevel research. The problem is the following: many macro–micro relations work within a relatively short time period, whereas many micro–macro relations require a longer-term perspective in order to be visible, and, hence, something that can be captured empirically (Kozlowski and Klein, 2000).

Since a microfoundational explanation in terms of Coleman's diagram calls for studying at least *Arrows 2* and *3* and potentially also *Arrow 1*, this asymmetry in the time that effects take to become visible needs to be considered when planning data collection. Thus, one may want to start the analysis at t = 0 with an account of how firm-level characteristics (e.g., organizational structure and control) influence the opportunities for action by organizational members at t = 1 (cf. Figure 3 in Section 3). But, if organization-level variables are only measured at t = 3, this is not feasible. This suggests that to fully make microfoundations 'come alive' empirically, other sampled data sets must be longitudinal and cover a sufficient time interval (or comprise sufficiently lagged data). Otherwise, if the time horizon is not sufficiently long, relations that do exist in reality may falsely be overlooked or rejected in an empirical study. Due to loss of respondents from one wave to another, collecting lagged or longitudinal data can be very difficult to implement in large sample studies. This is particularly the case if one wants to ensure sufficient variance of the variables, as we will discuss next when we highlight the challenges implied by microfoundations for sampling.

Achieving sufficient buy-in from key players or respondents in the organization(s) in order to overcome or prevent respondents participating in a first data collection but not willing to provide data again at a later stage (panel attrition) may be easier to achieve in smaller samples of selected organizations than in large samples. Therefore, in the context of microfoundational research, we believe small sample research ('case studies') can play a powerful role. Yet, whereas 'case studies' traditionally have a strong role in many research fields, they are somewhat 'looked down-upon' in other fields (or by 'quantitative' scholars), for their alleged inability to test causal claims due to a lack of sample size. This is due to how one defines causality and, consequently, what the necessary and sufficient conditions are for establishing it.

Usually, an important aspect of causality is the existence of a temporal sequence such that the presence of a particular phenomenon or outcome ('effect') follows the temporally prior presence of a certain factor ('cause'), and the absence of the effect follows the absence of the particular cause (e.g., Abell, 2011). Returning to our initial example from Section 1 about the different strategy theories that in different ways relate certain antecedents (causes) to firm outcomes and performance, testing upper echelons theory (Hambrick and Mason, 1984) would call for empirical data showing cases where superior firm performance ('effect') follows temporally the presence of a particular characteristic (or bundle of characteristics) within the firms' top management ('cause'), and where lack of superior performance (or low performance) temporally follows the absence of that top management characteristic (or set of characteristics). Provided careful functional specification of an empirical model (e.g., linear vs non-linear relationships), use of suitable controls (i.e., variables for other, potential factors relevant for the functional relationship of interest, such as – to stay in the example – the tools available to employees), such covariation as in our example can effectively be reconciled with causality (Abell, 2011; Pearl, 2009; Spirtes, Glymour, and Scheines, 2000). Hutzschenreuter and Horstkotte (2013) provide an example of such a study on the impact of demographic characteristics within upper echelons on decision-making and performance.

Quite obviously, such a reading of causality as statistical covariation implies a comparison of multiple cases (Abell, 2011; Ragin, 1992) – and, thus, requires that the sample is larger than one. Moreover, as basic inferential statistics teaches, given noise in most empirical data in practice (and even in laboratories due to the limited number of factors that can be tested in a single experiment), significantly more than two cases are typically necessary for ascertaining covariation at the commonly desired 'levels of confidence', like, for example, a 95 or 99 per cent 'confidence level', and thus to minimize the likelihood of falsely rejecting or accepting the presence of covariation among a cause and an effect. Consequently, seen this way, small sample research ('case studies') seems to violate an important prerequisite for establishing causality. Yet, such a reaction is too hasty.

As Abell (2009, 2011) outlines, if scholars are open to substitute this 'standard' approach of causal inference by what he calls *singular causality at the micro-level*, microfoundations research has a lot to gain from such small sample research. The concept of singular causality at the micro-level is less demanding in terms of the number of observations as it does not require the comparison of multiple cases, but allows causal relations to be supported by singular causal claims (e.g., 'Sally manipulated her revenue figures because of excessively high targets'). Such a singular causal claim can then, in a second step, when combined with other comparable claims (e.g., 'Francesco manipulated her revenue figures because of excessively high targets' or 'Nathalie didn't engage in manipulation because her targets are easy to achieve') be used to study whether or not (or to what extent) an explanation can be generalized (Abell, 2011). Thus, microfoundational research drawing on singular causality does not allow for immediately generalizable conclusions.[23] However, such narrative explanation can nonetheless serve a powerful function, whether formally (Abell, 2004) or informally specified. Thus, to sum up, as Abell (2011) and Abell, Foss, and Lyngsie (Empirical microfoundations for management research. Unpublished working paper, Copenhagen: Department of Strategic Management and Globalization, Copenhagen Business School.) note, drawing on the concept of singular causality allows research to accumulate across researchers, which, in turn, using the appropriate methods, permits testing the extent to which singular micro explanatory mechanisms can be generalized.

Moreover, small sample empirical research facilities studies of potentially very informative 'extremes', such as a company that exhibits strong performance even though it operates in an industry that, based on the SCP theory that we shortly outlined earlier, should show low profitability. Such 'outliers' can offer powerful insights into contingency factors or mediating variables so far unknown or 'Winsorized away' (discarded) within many traditional large sample analyses in order to make the distribution of observations fit the assumptions (notably the one of multi-normality) of standard ordinary least squares (OLS) regression (see McKelvey and Andriani (2005) on the need for discarding of extreme values). In fact, one could make the point that traditional large sample approaches draw in one form or the other on averages (such as minimizing the least squares in OLS regression), although scholars in much of management research, and in strategy research in particular, are (primarily) interested in identifying what makes organizations more successful (than the average) or protects them from falling 'below industry average' in performance. Small sample research ('case studies') can help better understand the nature of these extremes, their feasible origins, and their impact on

---

[23] It seems important to note, however, that one can well question the validity of the standard model of causality fuelled by data about the past. Thus, already Hume (1777) was very sceptical (to say the least) of the possibility – irrespective of the number of observations that one has – to empirically infer causality from (past) data (Glennan, 1996). Hence, the lack of immediate generalizability in the case of explanations drawing on the concept of singular causality may, in fact, weigh less heavily as commonly thought.

other individuals and organizations (Abell, Foss, and Lyngsie, unpublished working paper).

Sampling

Since microfoundational explanations span multiple analytical levels, empirically developing or testing theory from a microfoundations lens requires data that exhibits sufficient variability for the constructs of interest on *all* levels in the model in question. The collection of multilevel data, therefore, is often more painstaking and costly than single-level analyses (Kozlowski and Klein, 2000).

For example, in 2009 one of the authors of this volume paid a national statistics agency to conduct a survey on firm-level variables among the largest firms in a country and to link the survey data to a register with micro-level variables on the working population held by the agency. The idea was explicitly microfoundational: individual-level characteristics would offer insights in macro-level outcomes (such as innovation). Whereas the project has been successful in terms of publication, it is noteworthy that, for this service, the agency charged €100,000. This is a price that no PhD student can afford, and which also makes similar data-collection exercises challenging for most senior scholars.

If sampling is carried out based on the macro-level – such as, for example, the 500 largest firms in a country– then micro-level observations of, say, employees' skills, knowledge, attitudes, or character traits are not randomly drawn from a larger population (here: all employees in the country). Instead, they passively follow from the sample of macro-level observations. To stay in the example, since firms typically (carefully) select whom they hire and promote and since individuals who are dissatisfied with the (work) conditions at their employer tend to leave the firm, a firm's employees can rarely be considered to be a random sample of the overall population of the workforce in a country (Felin and Hesterly, 2007). This raises concerns regarding the representativeness and unbiasedness of the micro-level data.

Moreover, non-random micro-level sampling also confounds the direct effect of macro-level factors on micro-level antecedents with selection mechanisms (Abell, Foss, and Lyngsie, unpublished working paper). Sampling on the macro-level means that individual variation in micro-level factors cannot be directly reflected in macro-level outcomes, because macro-level outcomes reflect the combined effect of many individual-level antecedents and actions, rather than individual effects. This black boxes a key mechanism highlighted by microfoundations, namely that the effect of macro-level factors is mediated through individuals' actions (see Figure 1). Such black boxing means that the researcher is ignorant about the precise nature of the mechanism.

5.2 Analytical Methods for Microfoundations Research

Microfoundations and Traditional Regression-Based Methods

The dominant mode of empirical inquiry in macro management research is applying various regression-based techniques to large-scale, typically cross-sectional, data sets. Such approaches face problems of varying severity in the context of microfoundations (Abell, Foss, and Lyngsie, unpublished working paper; Aguinis and Molina-Azorin, 2015).

A basic challenge derives from the multilevel property of microfoundational explanations, which imply a nested data structure. For example, a scholar interested in firm innovativeness might predict that employees' explorative activities explain part of a firm's innovativeness. The scholar then would collect information on firm-level innovativeness – such as patent counts – and individual employees' explorative activities, such as, for example, how often they scan the environment for new technological trends or shifts in customer wishes. Except in the case of a firm with a single employee, such a study would imply that, for the micro-level in this microfoundational study, information from multiple employees per firm needs to be collected and analysed. As firms differ in whom they hire, retain, and promote, chances are good that the employees in a focal firm are not a random sample of the overall working population in a country (Felin and Hesterly, 2007). Rather, the scholar faces 'nested data'. The employees within the focal firm are more similar to each other than to the employees of another firm in terms of their skills, knowledge, motivations, personality traits, or some other factors. As a consequence, the responses from employees within a focal firm about, say their scanning behaviour, likely will be somewhat similar due to the similarities in their characteristics – that is, exhibit covariation. This makes it problematic to use analytical methods that assume independence of individual observations, such as standard OLS regression (e.g., Nezlek, 2008). Relying on such analytical methods in the presence of 'nested' data risks resulting in biased standard errors, which leads to increased Type I or Type II error rates when testing hypotheses (Aguinis and Molina-Azorin, 2015; Krasikova and LeBreton, 2019); that is, it makes it more likely, for example, that a hypothesis erroneously is considered to be supported by the data (i.e., that the null hypothesis is erroneously rejected) even though there it is not when one appropriately considers the nested nature of the data in the analysis.

Empirically, microfoundations research thus necessitates modelling the dependence caused by multilevel data structures (Aguinis and Edwards, 2014). This means – besides the need of sampling data on at least two different levels of analysis that we already discussed – deploying the appropriate statistical techniques to deal with the resulting data structures. Needless to say, this problem applies just as much to cases, like in our aforementioned example, where the 'micro' is the individual level and the 'macro' corresponds to the firm level as it does when the 'micro' or the 'macro' or both are located at other levels. 'Stacked' multilevel explanations, that is, models with more than two levels, in turn, obviously are just an 'extended version' of this challenge.

Analytically Relating the Micro to the Macro

As outlined earlier, when we introduced the Coleman 'bathtub', empirical analyses need to cover at least *Arrow 3* to qualify as 'microfoundational'. This implies that analyses purely focusing on the micro-level (*Arrow 2*), while certainly informative, do not suffice from a microfoundations lens. Only when combined with an analysis corresponding to *Arrow 3*, such analyses really help advance our understanding of how the macro-level phenomenon of interest evolves. Similarly, analyses focusing on *Arrow 1*, while covering multiple levels, are within a microfoundations lens insufficient if not combined with an analysis covering *Arrows 2* and *3* too. To be clear, both these kind of 'macrofoundations' for micro behaviour (*Arrow 1*) and the responses of individuals to micro-level behaviour (*Arrow 2*) are valuable, yet remain piecemeal for understanding macro phenomena (i.e., for explaining why we may observe *Arrow 4*) when not combined with an analysis relating the micro to the macro (*Arrow 3*). This is an important aspect to consider in assessing the suitability of various analytical methods in terms of what they can contribute to empirical microfoundations research.

Most notably, the fact that microfoundations emphasizes multiple analytical levels may be seen as simply calling for using an existent, quite popular method from multilevel research: hierarchical linear modelling (HLM). After all, HLM has many strengths, such as that it explicitly models both the micro- and macro-level random-error components, therefore recognizing 'that individuals within a group may be more similar to one another than they are to individuals in another group and may not, therefore, provide independent observations' (Hofmann, Griffin, and Gavin, 2000: 471). Not surprisingly, HLM has – under various labels – such as multilevel linear models (Goldstein, 1987), variance-components models (Longford, 1986), and random-coefficient models (Longford, 1993), become quite popular in recent years. Yet, in studies where the dependent variable (phenomenon of interest) is not at the lowest, that is, micro-level, 'then this approach will not usually be the most appropriate tool' (Hofmann, Griffin, and Gavin, 2000: 499). And, unfortunately, microfoundations per definition call for explaining a macro-level outcome *via* micro (lower-level) relations.

Thus, whereas HLM is a powerful tool for studies relating the macro to the micro, that is, covering *Arrows 1* and *2*, it is less suited to a core element of a microfoundations explanation: how the micro leads to the macro (Ployhart and Hendricks, 2019). That is, HLM is not geared towards work that, for example, 'asks about the extent to which individual-level characteristics influence or predict aggregate phenomena' (Hofmann, Griffin, and Gavin, 2000: 499).

Thus, if HLM is not the silver bullet for empirical microfoundations research, how can we deal with the '*Arrow 3* issue'? Here it is important to note that macro-level phenomena can emerge in two ways: composition, that is, 'phenomena that are essentially the same as they emerge upward across levels' (Kozlowski and Klein, 2000: 16), and compilation, which describes phenomena that comprise a common domain but are distinctively different as they emerge across levels' (ibid: 16). Moreover, building microfoundations for a macro phenomenon implies that we need methods that avoid throwing a carpet over the micro-level mechanisms (Abell, Foss, and Lyngsie, unpublished working paper).

Obviously, the simplest way of relating the micro- to the macro-level is through aggregation of the former based on averaging.[24] Based on these two criteria, such simple averaging may be suitable for certain micro-level attributes, but not for all, given the presence and the type of interactions and dependencies (Ostroff and Bowen, 2000). For example, simple averaging may be acceptable if variability within an organization is not an issue, but not if one expects that within-organization consensus is considered important for understanding the macro-level phenomenon. Similarly, averaging may lead to false conclusions about how generalizable within a firm some insights or phenomena are as, for example, the research on decreasing efficiency in larger teams suggest (Staats, Milkman, and Fox, 2012). Moreover, while averaging is easy to implement, it throws a carpet over the operation of micro-level mechanisms (Abell, Foss, and Lyngsie, unpublished working paper). Hence, aggregation by simple averaging does not do much to help advance empirical microfoundations research.

Diversity indices represent a moderate improvement to simple aggregation because they account for the dispersion of micro-level observations (Abell, Foss, and Lyngsie, unpublished working paper). However, diversity indices still do not directly capture micro–macro effects based on micro-level actions.

---

[24] Different forms of this averaging exist. Discussing these in more detail is beyond the scope of this volume. Mathieu and Luciano (2019) offer an excellent overview of the various averages approaches.

Furthermore, microfoundational analysis based on diversity indices may not yield results that can be clearly interpreted.[25]

Analytical methods relating the micro- to the macro-level that allow for capturing these cross-level effects are thus a key prerequisite for empirical microfoundations research to blossom. Moreover, such methods would help to bridge the micro and macro areas and their respective scholarly communities in management research (Eckardt et al., 2018). Much remains still to be done on the method side, but we would like to point out some methods that seem promising avenues: co-evolution networks, Bayesian narratives, agent-based models, and mixed methods research (Abell and Engel, 2018; Abell, Foss, and Lyngsie, unpublished working paper).

A promising large sample approach for studying the *Arrows 1* and *3* focuses attention upon the connection between covariation at two levels, while avoiding the dangers of ecological correlation (i.e., conflating individual and group-level correlations). It should also take into account that the micro-level typically involves strategically interacting, not independent, individuals (e.g., Milgrom and Roberts, 1992). One such approach focuses on the co-evolution in networks and aims at fostering our understanding of the underlying micro mechanisms that induce the evolution of social network structures on the macro-level (e.g., Burk, Steglich, and Snijders, 2007). Rather than standard regression techniques, which require independence of observations, co-evolution in networks explicitly accounts for covariation, notably, so-called actor covariates and dyadic covariates. The prior one refers to covariation among the characteristics of certain individuals (or groups of individuals), such as, when friends of two colleagues who are also friends become friends; the latter for covariation among the characteristics of pairs of individuals (or groups), like, for example, between the members of the sales department and those of the marketing department. Software like Siena (e.g., Burk, Steglich, and Snijders, 2007) facilitates implementing empirical analysis of co-evolution in networks. Yet, certain assumptions need to be considered when judging whether the approach is suitable to a particular microfoundational research question: first, these software allow the study of so-called complete networks, not personal (ego-centred) networks. That is, it is assumed that a set of individuals (nodes in the terminology of the approach) is given, and that (apart from some missing data) all links between these nodes are known. Second, they typically assume that the conditional probability distribution of future states depends exclusively upon the present state, not on the sequence of events that preceded it ('Markov property'). The

---

[25] If, however, one introduces the idea that the individual performances are distributed over an interaction structure, then it opens up the possibility of summarizing the properties the network so produced.

first assumption thus poses significant demands on the data quality used for the analysis; the second one hampers study of many real-world intra-organizational micro mechanisms, where history matters and parallel processes are important. Even more problematic, the emphasis is usually upon predictions at the micro-level, not the macro-level, which would require some summary concept which pictures the distribution of properties of nodes across a network (Abell, Foss, and Lyngsie, unpublished working paper).

Given the problem of matching the complexities of micro mechanisms with variation across macro units, Abell, Foss, and Lyngsie (unpublished working paper) point to the interplay of case studies conceived as Bayesian narratives involving singular causality and agent-based simulation as a promising approach for empirical microfoundations work. Bayesian narratives seek causal evidence through subjective counterfactuals – 'I would not have done that if that had not happened.' This approach seeks to establish tentative causal links and can provide a method of constructing case studies at the micro-level (Abell, 2011). Narratives are constructed from action-/decision-driven narrative paths, which account for the transformation of 'the world' from an initial state to a final state along chronologies of intervening states; parallel paths being permitted (Griffin, 1993; Heise, 1989). Such an approach facilitates looking beyond rational choice by highlighting the underlying beliefs and reasons for micro- and macro-level activity and behaviour (see Boudon, 2003). With a narrative approach the probity of each causal link is assessed using Bayesian methods, which estimate the odds for and against a link on the basis of the evidence collected.

Agent-based modelling, computational models, and other system simulation techniques help studying the emergent (macro) outcomes of the dynamics of simultaneously interacting (on a specified network/topology) rule-based micro agents as they allow tracing the implications of their behaviour for macro-level outcomes (e.g., Eckardt et al., 2018; Epstein, 2006; Mertens, Lorscheid, and Meyer, 2017). A well-known example of this approach is March's (1991) model of organizational learning, where slow and fast learners interact and jointly impact the organizations code and performance.

Narrative-based case studies can provide inputs to the construction of a simulation model, the empirical test of which is the generation of the variation of the macro outcome (Abell et al., 2014). In this context, narratives provide information into sequential interaction, that is, who interacts with and is influenced by whom (cf. Macy and Willer, 2002). Moreover, narrative analysis can be used to better understand the decision-making context that individuals in a simulation are placed in.

Combining narratives and simulation studies is an example of mixed methods. More generally, mixed methods are combinations of quantitative and qualitative research methods and promise that 'the systematic use of two methods offers contributions beyond those that single methods alone may produce' (Meuer and Rupietta, 2017: 324). Given the demands with respect to data and analytical procedure implied when studying microfoundations empirically, a combination of different methods seems a promising avenue to advance our understanding of many macro-level phenomena (Aguinis and Molina-Azorin, 2015). Typically, such research follows either a sequential or a concurrent (parallel) approach (Venkatesh, Brown, and Bala, 2013). In the case of a concurrent approach, such a multilevel mixed methods study may mean running a quantitative study at the micro-level (e.g., a classical survey or vignette experiment) and a qualitative one (based, for example, on interview data or organizational documents) at the macro-level. Drawing on the findings from both studies, such a multilevel mixed methods project would then develop overarching conclusions about the phenomenon of interest by triangulation of findings during the interpretation stage. A sequential multilevel mixed methods study, in contrast, might first rely on a quantitative study (e.g., using HLM) to spot specific cases (including, notably, some 'outliers') at the micro-level (individuals, groups, units, etc.). Subsequently, these specific cases and how their particular features and behaviours affect the macro-level could be studied in more detail using qualitative methods, such as in-depth longitudinal case studies using interviews and observations or action research. Given the sequential nature of such a project, results from the first stage can inform already the subsequent one (Meuer and Rupietta, 2017). Obviously, the inverse sequence of quantitative and qualitative also is possible. In line with such a sequential reasoning, Meuer and Rupietta (2017) recently proposed sequencing qualitative comparative analysis (QCA), a qualitative case-oriented method, with HLM. QCA uses Boolean algebra to compare combinations of conditions with reference to a predefined outcome and reveals alternative configurations (Ragin, 1987). It thus provides in-depth insights into the 'causal nature, and measuring nuanced degrees of set memberships (or "fit") of cases in configurations' (Meuer and Rupietta, 2017: 326)

6 Conclusions and Implications

6.1 Microfoundations: Good for Theory-Building

The push for microfoundations has become an important movement in management research over the last ten years or so. It has touched on and influenced research in a number of, mainly, macro management fields. It is a vibrant field with a fair amount of debate. Initial hostility is giving way to general acceptance. Partly, this is because microfoundations do not amount to an inherently constraining theory, but is a set of relatively broad and, in principle, is not very constraining for how to conduct research, theoretically as well as empirically. As we saw in the previous section, however, 'not very constraining' does not necessarily mean 'simple'. Thus, doing microfoundational empirical research is usually more demanding than running yet another regression based on a cross-section of variables derived from measuring at only the organizational level.

Microfoundations analysis has 'caught on', we think, because it manifests the basic scientific quest to explain more by digging deeper. As such, it is a manifestation of reductionism as a productive research practice. In this small volume, we have offered a number of illustrations of how making microfoundations explicit or tweaking existing microfoundations yield new insight. For example, much new insight in the workings of capabilities and routines has been obtained by being more explicit about their psychological underpinnings (e.g., Helfat and Peteraf, 2015; Salvato and Rerup, 2018). Similarly, new insight on the boundaries of the firm (e.g., Nickerson and Zenger, 2008) or choice of hierarchical form (e.g., Foss and Weber, 2016) has been obtained by offering more and new complementary microfoundational detail (in these cases relative to that offered by TCE). In strategy, behavioural strategy and strategic human capital have become flourishing subfields (e.g., Campbell, Coff, and Kryscynski, 2010; Campbell et al., 2010; Coff and Kryscynski, 2011; Gavetti, 2012). Thus, in particular on the theoretical domain, microfoundations has a positive proven track record. Successful empirical microfoundations work has been somewhat slower to emerge, but that is also changing as multilevel methods get increasingly diffused in the management research community, experiments have become a standard tool, and as micro data are becoming increasingly available.

6.2 Microfoundations: Good for Management Education

Besides fostering research that allows to better understand important (macro) phenomena, microfoundations promise to be good for what many of the readers of this Element do, namely teaching management theory and practice. A simple observation is that our teaching is inherently individual-centric. Thus, we educate students, that is, concrete individuals. We don't teach 'things' how they should affect other 'things'. And, if we tell students (we've done this) that 'capabilities cause high profitability' (or similar), we are lucky to have been blessed with inquisitive students who will ask, 'How? What do you mean?' – which inevitably takes us into microfoundational arguments.

More broadly, participant-centred learning calls for micro-level theorizing. The typical Harvard Business School case study features not only a decision dilemma, but also an individual who is placed in this dilemma and has to decide, act, and so on. Hence, it is not structure that decides or implies a certain performance. Rather, it is the manager in these cases who mediates the relation between the context and the subsequent behaviour of the organization. Thus, one particular advantage of a microfoundational approach to teaching is that it reminds students of *them* being the actor – and thus avoids blaming 'the system' or waiting for 'the system to solve problems'. It is thus in the spirit of free, self-responsible citizens, who do not need 'the system' (state, capitalism, or something else) to play the nanny for them.

Also, microfoundations helps in training students to understand that there are often no right answers, but that the 'right' answer depends on what one wants to do with this answer. That is, in some cases, an explanation of macroeconomic concepts by firm-level behaviour is sufficient (like in price theory), while, in other cases, one needs to go down to the individual and how she behaves, and yet, in other cases, some meso-level might be the right N-1 level. Hence, the microfoundations approach teaches students an important lesson: there is no universally appropriate lens for looking at the world of management; rather, the right lens/level to look at the world is contingent on the question that one asks.

6.3 Microfoundations: Good for Practice

When we teach executives and others with practical experience, we often find that they already speak a practical version of the language of microfoundations. The reason is the one identified by Chester Barnard (1938): managers cannot afford to leave individuals out of consideration, as so much management begins from individuals. Sure, managers may (and should) be deeply concerned about practices, systems, and structures (e.g., management information systems, cost allocation and transfer pricing practices, reward systems, criteria for promotion, and much else), but these practices still need to be designed with individuals, sometimes even concrete individuals, in mind. By the same token, managers' thinking may start from collective constructs (e.g., 'rival firms', 'suppliers', 'foreign markets', 'the competition', etc.), but any manager knows that these are abstract categories and that taking action, for example in response to 'the competition' or to penetrate a 'foreign market', depends on identifying and understanding much micro detail, including, for example, who is the CEO of the main competitor, how he or she has reacted in the past, what may be his or her intentions, and so on. Indeed, we think this basic insight is becoming perhaps even more practiced with the emergence over the last few decades of a set of influences often put under the 'knowledge economy' rubric (Foss, 2005; Foss and Linder, 2019).

One implication of the 'knowledge economy' is that what matters for competitive advantage is less economies of scale and scope per se (although these may still matter, e.g., to platform companies), but ultimately attracting, motivating, and retaining knowledge workers. SHRM looks into this, but we need to link it back to competitive advantage. This is what microfoundations research can do/is about. A related insight applies to stakeholder management, which is inherently challenging because it is shot through with micro details regarding the relative importance of various stakeholder groups, how they are composed and how they react, who the key individuals are, what their motives and thoughts are, and so on. Here, the devil is literally in the details. Bottom line: clever practice is inherently microfoundational!

Of course, consultants know this. Consulting is a way to change how firms operate and is done by individuals consulting other individuals (clients) – and, hence, knowing how the recommendations enhance competitive advantage is key. After all, strategy consulting firms at the end live off the belief that such individual-level actions change the competitive position of firms. At the same time, it is also true that the major consulting houses earn a living by peddling 'best practices'. Indeed, best practices do exist, even if they are highly generic (Bloom and van Reenen, 2007). Most practices need adaptation, reflecting not only the unique qualities of the firms in which they will be implemented, but also the organizational members. Microfoundations may be interpreted as issuing a warning to practitioners, namely that it may be dangerous to believe that 'best practices' or 'most admired companies' are what one should simply follow.

Finally, microfoundations may be a useful bridge between research and practice. Practitioners often have little patience with the typical piece of management research, involving large samples, measuring primarily at the organizational level, and involving often sophisticated statistical methods. And, indeed, the practice implications of such research may often seem remote. Because microfoundational research inherently involves linking levels, is predisposed towards individuals and their interactions, and appeals to causal mechanisms, it has the potential to speak directly face-to-face to practitioners. In fact, microfoundations may be one way in which so-called action-based research – which has had a somewhat deserved problematic reputation because of issues with biases and generalizability – may regain respectability.

6.4 The Future of Microfoundations in Management Research

As we have been almost at pains to emphasize in this volume, microfoundations is a broad tent. It imposes rather few restrictions on research efforts. We consider that this should imply that management scholars holding quite different perspectives (or different views of how empirical inquiry is best pursued) may all subscribe to the microfoundations agenda. And we think that the microfoundations movement will continue to be influential and even grow in strength in management research. The fundamental reason is that much management research is still characterized by reification of collective constructs and appeal to macro causation, which are ruled out by microfoundations, and much management research has unclear microfoundations and fails to account for inter-level relations in a convincing manner. In short, there is still much to do from a microfoundational perspective.

It is perhaps not surprising that microfoundations were first launched as a theme and first impacted the field in management research that is most heavily influenced by economics, namely strategy (Felin and Foss, 2005; Gavetti, 2005). Economics has a history of microfoundational discussion, and virtually all economists accept the need for furnishing microfoundations. For example, the discussion of what are proper microfoundations for macroeconomics has raged since the 1960s (Janssen, 2005; Weintraub, 1979). However, management fields that have not been much influenced by economics are moving towards embracing microfoundations because these represent meaningful opportunities for research. A case in point is work on 'new institutionalism' in organizational analysis, which is fundamentally a sociological enterprise. The emphasis is very strongly on context and practices shaping beliefs and behaviours. To the extent that levels are explicitly theorized, it is the top-down (downward causation) link from context and practices to individual behaviours that are emphasized. However, recent work in this field (e.g., Cardinale, 2018) increasingly seeks to challenge and extend its microfoundations, for example, by allowing actors to act strategically (and not just following the rules suggested by institutions) under the constraints represented by institutions or even work to change the institutions themselves or introduce new institutions (as in work on 'institutional entrepreneurship' (Battilana, Leca, and Boxenbaum, 2009)). Thus, it is entirely possible for sociologists, who have traditionally been sceptical of 'reductionism', 'methodological individualism', and so on to embrace microfoundations.

While this example illustrates the broad tent nature of microfoundations, it also suggests that it is probably unrealistic to expect that the microfoundations movement in management itself will give rise to unified microfoundations (cf. Felin et al., 2005) – that is, commonly held theory with clearly delineated and generally accepted behavioural assumptions, generally agreed upon inter-level mechanisms, or agreed upon empirical research methods. This is something that may be achieved in the disciplines. For example, economics gets close to this picture of a unified field. However, management is an amalgam of insights from many different fields, and much of what happens in management with regard to insights in behaviour, empirical research methodology, and so on is driven by what happens in the disciplines. There are indeed various indications that the hitherto very different views of man held in disciplines such as sociology, economics, and psychology are converging, as, for example, sociologists and psychologists increasingly appreciate the role of constraints in decision-making and as (behavioural) economists increasingly include more sophisticated models of reasoning and of how environmental cues shape our decisions. This suggests that one should expect work in management on micro-foundations to be 'opportunistic' and pragmatic, drawing on whatever useful ideas are offered by the disciplines. This prediction has little to do with microfoundations per se, and a lot to do with the nature of management as a research area.

So, what may those new problems be that management scholars may wish to address from a microfoundational perspective? Obviously, we are influenced by our own backgrounds in strategy, entrepreneurship, and management control, and we certainly do not claim that the following new problems are necessarily the most compelling, but here are some illustrative problems, in addition to those mentioned previously in this volume (i.e., CSR's impact on organizational goals (Section 3) or institutions (this section)).[26]

Do Heuristics and Biases Scale Up?

The vast heuristics and biases literature (now partially overlapping with research on 'dual processing') points to a mind-boggling number of ways in which the use of heuristics in decision-making may lead to decision-making errors. It is much less clear how such biases aggregate up (Fehr and Tyran, 2005). This is an excellent opportunity to examine the difference between aggregation processes (i.e., *Arrow 3* of the Coleman diagram; see Figure 1, Section 2) that work by 'composition' (i.e., 'more of the same') and processes (of 'compilation') that imply some sort of discontinuity, that is, the emergence of a new, qualitatively different characteristic in the aggregate (cf. Kozlowski and Klein, 2000: 16). Some research on this matter already

---

[26] For discussion of microfoundations in the context of family business research, see de Massis and Foss (2018).

exists (e.g., Fehr and Tyran, 2005), but more such research would seem to be particularly pertinent in the cases of ideation processes, consensus formation, and political processes in general in organizations. Along the same line, yet across organizational boundaries, one may wonder how such biases scale up in cases where two or more organizations collaborate, such as, in the case of joint audits. Governments in various countries, among others, Denmark and France, require or required that a firm's financial statements are audited by two separate audit firms (respectively, obviously, the teams of auditors within these audit firms). The rationale typically given for this is that such joint audits should lead to higher audit quality – and, hence, better quality of financial statements than audits carried out by only one audit firm. Research has started looking into whether this is actually true in practice, yet offers mixed evidence (e.g., Deng et al., 2014; Ratzinger-Sakel et al., 2013; Zerni et al., 2012). This may be partially due to a focus on audit firm-level variables (e.g., size of the audit firms), rather than more micro aspects, such as the pair of audit team or individual audit partner interactions and their characteristics. Therefore, microfoundations research studying whether and how individual-level cognitive biases of auditors aggregate to audit team and then to pairs of auditors (and audit firms), getting amplified or not, would seem a highly relevant research field, both for further theory building and for policymakers.

Behaviours, Governance Costs, and Organizational Choice

We have highlighted the economics of organization (i.e., agency theory, TCE, etc.) as one of the explicitly microfoundational source theories of management research. However, this body of theory also employs behavioural assumptions that are either quite controversial (e.g., opportunism) or relatively vaguely described (e.g., bounded rationality). Partly this is what gives them their 'cutting power'. However, much additional insights into the costs of governance and, therefore, organizational choice may be obtained by putting richer behavioural assumptions into these theories. Some steps into this direction have already been made. For example, Hendry (2002) extends agency theory – and the conclusions that can be drawn for organizing work – by allowing for honest, but 'incompetent' agents. Linder, Foss, and Stea (2017) explore how a more realistic account of the human capacity to read other people's desires, intentions, knowledge, and beliefs – that is, to have individuals differ in their theory of someone else's mind, rather than just assuming blatant (binary) information asymmetry – allows the refinement of agency theory's insights. Nickerson and

Zenger (2008), in turn, examine the organizational consequences of envy costs and show that the inclusion of such costs helps in the understanding of wage compression and hierarchical choice. Similarly, Foss and Weber (2016) show how the inclusion of richer models of bounded rationality in TCE allows for new insight into hierarchical choice. Lindenberg and Foss (2011) and Foss and Lindenberg (2013), in turn, extend the discussion of motivation and incentives in organizations by relaxing the assumption of all individuals being all the time opportunistic. These authors assume, however, that forms that minimize the costs of envy or bounded rationality will be chosen. In fact, organizational choice itself may be influenced by bounded rationality. In other words, part of the microfoundations of organization design is understanding the choices of organization designers.

Nudges in Organizations

Relatedly, a third possible theme concerns the behavioural economics/psychology foundations of decision-making in organizations (Powell, Lovallo, and Fox, 2011). For many years, there has been a discussion in public policy research (e.g., Thaler and Sunstein, 2008) concerning the role of small and inexpensive 'nudges' in shaping large-scale improvements in individual welfare and collective decision-making (Thaler and Sunstein, 2008). Similarly, in firms or other organizations, simple interventions might constrain or enable individual-level factors (cf. Heath, Larrick, and Klayman, 1998) and, therefore, affect how different individual-level propensities, biases, and heuristics are manifest in organizational contexts. Thus, recent research has begun to explore how 'choice architectures' and information presentation have important implications for decision quality (e.g., Besedeš et al., 2015; Cardinaels and van Veen-Dirks, 2010; Homburg, Artz, and Wieseke, 2012; Münscher, Vetter, and Scheuerle, 2015). For example, Besedeš et al. (2015) show how choice architectures that restrict choice contribute to better decisions by reducing information overload. Cardinaels and van Veen-Dirks (2010), in turn, demonstrate that simple changes in the presentation of performance metrics in internal reporting affect the weight decision makers put on financial versus non-financial indicators. More research that identifies how the presentation and interface of choices, the order of choices, defaults, incentives, and other factors affect information processing and decision quality seems like a promising avenue by which microfoundations research can enhance our understanding of firm's actions, facilitate teaching, and enable managers to architecture their organization's systems in such a way as to improve organizational decision-making.

Corruption

About ten years ago, electrics and electronics giant Siemens made it to the headlines for what was one of the largest corruption scandals in the world. Yet, corruption is a widespread phenomenon and, not surprisingly, it regularly attracts attention from policymakers and business scholars. Among others, research has looked into country-level causes and consequences of corruption (Lambsdorff, 2007; Paldam, 2002; Steidlmeier, 1999), the role of organizational characteristics like organizational culture (e.g., Anand, Ashford, and Joshi 2004) and different forms of accountability for corruption (Serra, 2011). A small stream of work has also looked into the role of socio-demographic characteristics of the briber or bribee – notably, gender, age, or an individual's cultural background (Barr and Serra, 2010; Cameron et al., 2009; Fišar et al. 2016). All the latter work highlights the importance of considering individual differences for better understanding corruption. Yet, to our knowledge, so far no work exists that pulls the insights gained at various levels together and looks into cross-level relationships to shed more light on how and why respected and renowned corporations, like Siemens, can get dragged deeper and deeper into corruption. Since corruptive behaviours of individuals and organizations lead to numerous negative consequences, such as, reduced economic development, lower public trust in institutions, or biased income distribution in societies, we believe that building microfoundations for corruption is of high practical relevance.

Heterogeneity in Internal Control

Not only in the case of the corruption scandal at Siemens, but in many corporate scandals, the media is quick to point towards weaknesses in a firm's 'internal controls'. And in many cases, it rightly is so. Thus, for example, in the 2008 case of junior trader Jerôme Kerviel inflicting Société Générale a multibillion Euro trading loss, the firm's internal control (respectively, their weakness) seems to have played a crucial role. This raises the questions of what distinguishes defunct from well-functioning internal control and how firms end up with either of them. Bedford, Malmi, and Sandelin (2016) recently empirically showed that there are multiple ways by which firms can combine individual control practices and that some of these combinations are more effective than others given interdependencies between individual control tools and practices. While their study and other work exploring combinations of individual control tools and practices as 'packages' or 'systems' (e.g., Grabner and Moers, 2013; Linder et al., 2015; Malmi and Brown, 2008) thus suggest significant heterogeneity in firm's internal controls and that such heterogeneity matters for firm behaviour and performance, little is known about the microfoundations of this heterogeneity. That is, what are the microfoundations that help explain whether an organization chooses combination A over combination B of individual control tools and practices? And how do combinations A and B differ in their effects? More knowledge in this field can enhance our understanding of firms' internal control practices and, thus, facilitate teaching, inform shareholders, and/or public policymakers about potential needs to mandate certain combinations of control tools and practices to be used (or avoided), and enable managers to check whether their organization's internal controls are suboptimal.

Capabilities and Strategic Human Capital

It is fitting to end where the microfoundations discussion in management began, namely with the microfoundations of capabilities and other firm-specific knowledge assets that are highlighted in various macro management literatures (e.g., competences, dynamic capabilities, absorptive capacity, etc.). As late as 2010, Foss, Husted, and Michailova (2010) could document a strong macro bias in the 'knowledge' literature in strategy and organization. Indeed, significant progress has been made here, however, as witnessed by some of the literature streams we have discussed, such as the strategic human capital stream of research. Much of this literature has been taken up with issues of the links between human capital specificity, bargaining, and value appropriation, but it does have the potential to illuminate our understanding of capabilities in important ways. For example, Raffiee and Coff (2016) find that organizational commitment and, to some extent, tenure are negatively related to employee perceptions of the firm-specificity of their knowledge and that employer-provided on-the-job training is unrelated to perceived firm-specificity. This raises the interesting question whether firm capabilities are really perceived as distinctive within a firm or actually underestimated – and therefore have a tendency to erode over time (the firm does not sufficiently 'fight' for keeping knowledgeable employees or may even engage in activities that the employees may consider reduce relation specificity of their knowledge). More generally, linking human capital to the emergence, maintenance, decay, and so on of firm-level capability is an exciting agenda for strategic human capital research.

Capabilities and the Multinational Firm

A dominant theory in international management asserts that the multinational firm exists by virtue of its superior ability to build distinctive, valuable capabilities on the basis of knowledge inputs sourced at a variety of geographical locations (Kogut and Zander, 1993). In an early essay, Foss and Pedersen (2004) argued that this literature was essentially devoid of microfoundations. They later (Foss and Pedersen, 2019) scrutinize the literature, analysing fifty-two papers published in twelve top journals on knowledge in multinational firms. They find that none of the analysed articles proffer microfoundations in the sense of theoretically or empirically identifying the intra- and inter-level mechanisms indicated by the Coleman diagram. There are partial analyses (e.g., analysis of top-down relations), but not a single example of a full microfoundational explanation. However, as Foss and Pedersen (2019) illustrate, there are plenty of opportunities for work in this space, for example, with respect to not only better understanding the dynamics (emergence, maintenance, transformation, etc.) of those knowledge assets that may truly differentiate multinational firms, but also regarding con-structs such as 'psychic distance' (firms are not different from each other in terms of such distance – individuals are).

6.5 Coda

Management research has long been characterized by a micro and macro divide. It wasn't always so. The classical thinkers that helped found and shape manage-ment research – Chester Barnard and Herbert Simon come to mind – saw the understanding of organizations as ultimately rooted in the understanding of decisions. To be sure, decisions are taken in a context and decision-making in organizations is organizational decision-making. But, this is not at variance with microfoundations, which indeed allows for contextual, structural, and so on influences on decision-making, as we have repeatedly argued. The question of when the micro–macro divide got established in management research is a subject that is worthy of a major independent study. However, our basic overall point in this small volume is that for many explanatory purposes we need to overcome this divide, and, as it were, return to Barnard and Simon. Microfoundations is an important step in that direction.

References

Abell, P. (2004). Narrative explanation: An alternative to variable-centered explanation? *Annual Review of Sociology*, 30, 287–310.

Abell, P. (2009). A case for cases. *Sociological Methods and Research*, 32, 1–33.

Abell, P. (2011). Singular mechanisms and Bayesian narratives, in Demeulenaere, P. (ed.). *Analytical Sociology and Social Mechanisms*. Cambridge: Cambridge University Press, 121–35.

Abell, P., and Engel, O. (2018). *The Coleman Diagram, Small N Inquiry and Ethnographic Causality*. Working Paper, London: London School of Economics.

Abell, P., Felin, T., and Foss, N. (2008). Building microfoundations for the routines, capabilities, and performance links. *Managerial and Decision Economics*, 29, 489–502.

Agassi, J. (1960). Methodological individualism. *British Journal of Sociology*, 11, 244–70.

Aggarwal, V., Posen, H. E., and Workiewicz, M. (2017). Adaptive capacity to technological change: A microfoundational approach. *Strategic Management Journal*, 38, 1212–31.

Aguinis, H., Boyd, B. K., Pierce, C. A., and Short, J. C. (2011). Walking new avenues in management research methods and theories: Bridging micro and macro domains. *Journal of Management*, 37, 395–403.

Aguinis, H., and Edwards, J. R. (2014). Methodological wishes for the next decade and how to make wishes come true. *Journal of Management Studies*, 51, 143–74.

Aguinis, H., and Molina-Azorin, J. F. (2015). Using multilevel modeling and mixed methods to make theoretical progress in microfoundations for strategy research. *Strategic Organization*, 13, 353–64.

Aime, F., Johnson, S., and Ridge, J. W. (2010). The routine may be stable but the advantage is not: Competitive implications of key employee mobility. *Strategic Management Journal*, 31, 75–87.

Anand, V., Ashford, B. E., Joshi, M. (2004). Business as usual: The acceptance and perpetuation of corruption in organizations. *Academy of Management Perspectives*, 18(2), 9–23.

Argote, L., and Ren, Y. (2012). Transactive memory systems: A microfoundation of dynamic capabilities. *Journal of Management Studies*, 49, 1375–82.

Asher, C. C., Mahoney, J. M., and Mahoney, J. T. (2005). Towards a property rights foundation for stakeholder theory of the firm. *Journal of Management and Governance*, 9, 5–32.

Baer, M., Dirks, K. T., and Nickerson, J. A. (2013). Microfoundations of strategic problem formulation. *Strategic Management Journal*, 34, 197–214.

Bain, J. S. (1959). *Industrial Organization: A Treatise*. New York: John Wiley.

Bapuji, H., Hora, M., and Saeed, A. M. (2012). Intentions, intermediaries, and interaction: Examining the emergence of routines. *Journal of Management Studies*, 49, 1586–607.

Barnard, C. (1938). *Functions of the Executive*. Boston: Harvard University Press.

Barnett, M. L. (2007). Stakeholder influence capacity and the variability of financial returns to corporate social responsibility. *Academy of Management Review*, 32(3), 794–816.

Barney, J. B. (1991). Firm resources and sustained competitive advantage. *Journal of Management*, 17, 99–121.

Barney, J. B., and Felin, T. (2013). What are microfoundations? *Academy of Management Perspectives*, 27, 138–55.

Barr, A., and Serra, D. (2010). Corruption and culture: An experimental analysis. *Journal of Public Economics*, 94(11–12), 862–69.

Battilana, J., Leca, B., and Boxenbaum, E. (2009). How actors change institutions: Towards a theory of institutional entrepreneurship. *The Academy of Management Annals*, 3(1), 65–107.

Bedford, D. S., Malmi, T., and Sandelin, M. (2016). Management control effectiveness and strategy: An empirical analysis of packages and systems. *Accounting, Organizations and Society*, 51, 12–28.

Besedeš, T., Deck, C., Sarangi, S., and Shor, M. (2015). Reducing choice overload without reducing choices. *Review of Economics and Statistics*, 97(4), 793–802.

Bitektine, A., and Haack, P. (2015). The "macro" and the "micro" of legitimacy: Toward a multilevel theory of the legitimacy process. *Academy of Management Review*, 40(1), 49–75.

Bloom, N. and van Reenen, J. (2007). Measuring and explaining management practices across countries. *Quarterly Journal of Economics*, 144: 1351–408.

Boudon, R. (2003). Beyond rational choice theory. *Annual Review of Sociology*, 29, 1–21.

Bridoux, F., Coeurderoy, R., and Durand, R. (2017). Heterogeneous social motives and interactions: The three predictable paths of capability development. *Strategic Management Journal*, 38(9), 1755–73.

Bridoux, F., and Stoelhorst, J. (2014). Microfoundations for stakeholder theory: Managing stakeholders with heterogeneous motives. *Strategic Management Journal*, 35, 107–25.

Burchell, S., Clubb, C., Hopwood, A., Hughes, J., and Nahapiet, J. (1980). The roles of accounting in organizations and society. *Accounting, Organizations and Society*, 5(1), 5–27.

Burk, W. J., Steglich, C. E. G., and Snijders, T. A. B. (2007). Beyond dyadic interdependence: Actor-oriented models for co-evolving social networks and individual behaviors. *International Journal of Behavioral Development*, 31(4), 397–404.

Cameron, L., Chaudhuri, A., Erkal, N., and Gangadharan, L. (2009). Propensities to engage in and punish corrupt behavior: Experimental evidence from Australia, India, Indonesia and Singapore. *Journal of Public Economics*, 93(7–8), 843–51.

Campbell, B. A., Coff, R., and Kryscynski, D. (2010). Rethinking sustained competitive advantage from human capital. *Academy of Management Review*, 37, 376–95.

Campbell, B. A., Ganco, M., Franco, A. M., and Agarwal, R. (2010). Who leaves, where to, and why worry? Employee mobility, entrepreneurship and effect on source firm performance. *Strategic Management Journal*, 33, 65–87.

Cardinaels, E., and van Veen-Dirks, P. M. G. (2010). Financial versus non-financial information: The impact of information organization and presentation in a balanced scorecard. *Accounting, Organizations and Society*, 35, 565–78.

Cardinale, I. (2018). Beyond constraining and enabling: Toward new microfoundations for institutional theory. *Academy of Management Review*, 43, 132–55.

Carroll, A. B. (1999). Corporate social responsibility: evolution of a definitional construct. *Business & Society*, 38(3), 268–95.

Chadwick, I. C., and Raver, J. L. (2015). Motivating organizations to learn: Goal orientation and its influence on organizational learning. *Journal of Management*, 41(3), 957–86.

Cho, C. H., Michelon, G., Patten, D. M., and Roberts, R. W. (2015). CSR disclosure: The more things change … ? *Accounting, Auditing & Accountability Journal*, 28(1), 14–35.

Coff, R., and Kryscynski, D. (2011). Drilling for micro-foundations of human capital-based competitive advantages. *Journal of Management*, 37, 1429–43.

Cohen, M. (2012). Perceiving and remembering routine action: Fundamental micro-level origins. *Journal of Management Studies*, 49(8), 1383–8.

Coleman, J. (1990). *Foundations of Social Theory*. Boston: Harvard University Press.

Craver, C. F. (2007). *Explaining the Brain: Mechanisms and the Mosaic Unity of Neuroscience*. Oxford: Oxford University Press.

Crook, R. T., Todd, S. Y., Combs, J. G., Woehr, D. J., and Ketche, D. J., Jr (2011). Does human capital matter? A meta-analysis of the relationship between human capital and firm performance. *Journal of Applied Psychology*, 96(3), 443–56.

Cyert, R. M., and March, J. G. (1963). *A Behavioral Theory of the Firm*. Englewood Cliffs, NJ: Prentice Hall.

Dai, Y., Roundy, P. T., Chok, J. I., Ding, F., and Byun, G. (2016). 'Who knows what?' in new venture teams: Transactive memory systems as a micro-foundation of entrepreneurial orientation. *Journal of Management Studies*, 53, 1320–47.

Debreu, G. (1959). *Theory of Value: An Axiomatic Analysis of Economic Equilibrium*. New Haven, CT: Yale University Press.

de Massis, A., and Foss, N. J. (2018). Advancing family business research: The promise of microfoundations. *Family Business Review*, 31(4), 386–96.

Deng, M., Lu, T., Simunic, D. A., and Ye, M. (2014). Do joint audits improve or impair audit quality? *Journal of Accounting Research*, 52, 1029–60.

Denyer, D., and Tranfield, D. (2008). Producing a systematic review, in Buchanan, D. (ed.). *The Sage Handbook of Organization Research Methods*. London: Sage, 671–89.

Dessein, W., Galeotti, A., and Santos, T. (2016). Rational inattention and organizational focus. *American Economic Review*, 106(6), 1522–36.

Dassein, W., and Santos, T. (2006). Adaptive organizations. *Journal of Political Economy*, 114(5), 956–95.

Devinney, T. (2009). Is the socially responsible corporation a myth? The good, the bad, and the ugly of corporate social responsibility. *Academy of Management Perspectives*, 23, 44–56.

Devinney, T. (2013). Is microfoundational thinking critical to management thought and practice? *Academy of Management Perspectives*, 27, 81–4.

Donaldson, T., and Preston, L. E. (1995). The stakeholder theory of the corporation: concepts, evidence, and implications. *Academy of Management Review*, 20(1), 65–91.

Dyllick, T., and Hockerts, K. (2002). Beyond the business case for corporate sustainability. *Business Strategy and the Environment*, 11(2), 130–41.

Ebers, M., and Maurer, I. (2014). Connections count: How relational embeddedness and relational empowerment foster absorptive capacity. *Research Policy*, 43, 318–32.

Eckardt, R., Crocker, A., Ahn, Y., et al. (2018). Reflections on the micro-macro divide: Ideas from the trenches and moving forward. *Strategic Organization*, 17(3), 385–402.

Eisenhardt, K., Furr, N. R., and Bingham, C. B. (2010). Microfoundations of performance: Balancing efficiency and flexibility in dynamic environments. *Organization Science*, 21, 1263–73.

Elster, J. (1989). *Nuts and Bolts for the Social Sciences*. Cambridge: Cambridge University Press.

Epstein, J. M. (2006). *Generative Social Science: Studies in Agent-Based Computational Modeling*. Princeton, NJ: Princeton University Press.

Epstein, B. (2015). *The Ant Trap: Rebuilding the Foundations of the Social Sciences*. Oxford: Oxford University Press.

Fehr, E., and Tyran, J. R. (2005). Individual rationality and aggregate outcomes. *Journal of Economic Perspectives*, 19, 43–66.

Felin, T., and Foss, N. (2005). Strategic organization: A field in search of micro-foundations. *Strategic Organization*, 3, 441–55.

Felin, T., and Foss, N. (2006). Individuals and organizations: Thoughts on a microfoundations project for strategic management and organizational analysis. *Research Methodology in Strategy and Management*, 3, 253–88.

Felin, T., and Foss, N. (2011). The endogenous origins of organizational experience, routines and capabilities: The poverty of stimulus. *Journal of Institutional Economics*, 7, 231–56.

Felin, T., and Foss, N. (2012). The (proper) microfoundations of routines and capabilities: A response to Winter, Pentland, Hodgson and Knudsen. *Journal of Institutional Economics*, 8, 271–88.

Felin, T., Foss, N., Heimeriks, K., and Madsen, T. (2012). Microfoundations of routines and capabilities: Individuals, processes, and structure. *Journal of Management Studies*, 49, 1351–74.

Felin, T., Foss, N.J., and Ployhart, R. (2015). The microfoundations movement in strategy and organization theory. *The Academy of Management Annals*, 9(1), 575–632.

Felin, T., and Hesterly, W. (2007). The knowledge-based view, nested heterogeneity, and new value creation: Philosophical considerations on the locus of knowledge. *Academy of Management Review*, 32, 195–218.

Felin, T., and Spender, J.-C. (2009). An exchange of ideas about knowledge governance: Seeking first principles and microfoundations, in Foss, N. J., and Michailova, S. (eds), *Knowledge Governance: Processes and Perspectives*. Oxford: Oxford University Press, 247–71.

Felin, T., and Zenger, T. R. (2011). Information aggregation, matching and radical market–hierarchy hybrids: Implications for the theory of the firm. *Strategic Organization*, 9, 163–73.

Fišar, M., Kubák, M., Špalek, J., and Tremewan, J. (2016). Gender differences in beliefs and actions in a framed corruption experiment. *Journal of Behavioral and Experimental Economics*, 63, 69–82.

Foss, N. J. (2003). Selective intervention and internal hybrids: Interpreting and learning from the rise and decline of the Oticon spaghetti organization. *Organization Science*, 14, 331–49.

Foss, N. J. (2005). *Strategy, Economic Organization, and the Knowledge Economy: The Coordination of Firms and Resources*. Oxford: Oxford University Press.

Foss, N. J. (2012). Theory of science perspectives on strategic management: Debates and a novel view, in Dagnino, G. B. (ed.), *Elgar Handbook of Research on Competitive Strategy*. Cheltenham: Edward Elgar.

Foss, N. J., Husted, K., and Michailova, S. (2010). Governing knowledge sharing in organizations: Levels of analysis, governance mechanisms and research directions. *Journal of Management Studies*, 47(3), 455–82.

Foss, N. J., and Lindenberg, S. (2013). Micro-foundations for strategy: A goal-framing perspective on the drivers of value creation. *Academy of Management Perspectives*, 27, 85–102.

Foss, N. J., Lindenberg, S. M., and Weber, L. L. (2019). Employees behaving badly: How opportunism differs across hierarchical forms (and how to handle it). *Academy of Management Proceedings*, 2019(1), https://doi.org/10.5465/AMBPP.2019.15882abstract.

Foss, N. J., and Linder, S. (2019). The changing nature of the corporation and the economic theory of the firm, in: Clarke, T., O'Brien, J., and O'Kelley, C. (eds), *The Oxford Handbook of the Corporation*. Oxford: Oxford University Press, 539–61.

Foss, J. N., and Lyngsie, J. (2017). The more, the merrier? Women in top-management teams and entrepreneurship in established firms. *Strategic Management Journal*, 38(3), 484–505.

Foss, N. J., and Pedersen, T. (2004). Governing knowledge processes in the multinational corporation. *Journal of International Business Studies*, 35(5), 339–49.

Foss, N. J., and Pedersen, T. (2019). Microfoundations in international management research: Individuals and contextual determinants of knowledge sharing in multinational corporations. *Journal of International Business Studies* (forthcoming).

Foss, N. J., and Weber, L. (2016). Moving opportunism to the back seat: Bounded rationality, costly conflict, and hierarchical forms. *Academy of Management Review*, 41(1), 61–79.

Freeman, R. E. (1994). The politics of stakeholder theory: some future directions. *Business Ethics Quarterly*, 4, 409–21.

Freeman, R. E., and Evan, W. M. (1990). Corporate governance: A stakeholder interpretation. *Journal of Behavioral Economics*, 19(4), 337–59.

Freeman, R. E., Wicks, A. C., and Parmar, B. (2004). Stakeholder theory and 'The corporate objective revisited'. *Organization Science*, 15(3), 364–69.

Friedland, R., and Alford, R. R. (1991). Bringing society back in: Symbols, practices and institutional contradictions, in: Powell, W. W., and DiMaggio, P. J. (eds), *The New Institutionalism in Organizational Analysis*. Chicago: The University of Chicago Press, 232–63.

Garriga, E., and Melé, D. (2004). Corporate social responsibility theories: mapping the territory. *Journal of Business Ethics*, 53, 51–71.

Gavetti, G. (2005). Cognition and hierarchy: Rethinking the microfoundations of capabilities' development. *Organization Science*, 16, 599–617.

Gavetti, G. (2012). Toward a behavioral theory of strategy. *Organization Science*, 23(1), 267–85.

Glennan, S. (1996). Mechanisms and the nature of causation. *Erkenntnis*, 44, 49–71.

Goldstein, H. (1987). *Multilevel Models in Educational and Social Research*. New York: Oxford University Press.

Gottschalg, O., and Zollo, M. (2007). Interest alignment and competitive advantage. *Academy of Management Review*, 32(2), 418–37.

Grabner, I., and Moers, F. (2013). Management control as a system or a package? Conceptual and empirical issues. *Accounting, Organizations and Society*, 38(6–7), 407–19.

Griffin, L. J. (1993). Narrative, event-structure analysis, and causal interpretation in historical sociology. *The American Journal of Sociology*, 98(5), 1094–133.

Grigoriou, K., and Rothaermel, F. T. (2014). Structural microfoundations of innovation: The role of relational stars. *Journal of Management*, 40(2), 586–615.

Haas, M. R., and Cummings, J. N. (2015). Barriers to knowledge seeking within MNC teams: Which differences matter most?*Journal of International Business Studies*, 46(1), 36–62.

Hallberg, N. L. (2017). The micro-foundations of pricing strategy in industrial markets: A case study in the European packaging industry. *Journal of Business Research*, 76, 179–88.

Hambrick, D. C., and Mason, P. A. (1984). Upper echelons: The organization as a reflection of its top managers. *Academy of Management Review*, 9(2), 193–206.

Harmon, D., Haack, P., and Roulet, T. J. (2019). Microfoundations of institutions: A matter of structure vs. agency or level of analysis? *Academy of Management Review*, 44(2), 464–7.

Harrison, J. S., Bosse, D. A., and Phillips, R. A. (2010). Managing for stakeholders, stakeholder utility functions, and competitive advantage. *Strategic Management Journal*, 3, 58–74.

Hart, O. (1995). Corporate governance: Some theory and implications. *The Economic Journal*, 105, 678–89.

Hayek, F. (1973). *Law, Legislation, and Liberty*, vol. 1: Rules and Order. Chicago: University of Chicago Press.

Heath, C., Larrick, R. P., and Klayman, J. (1998). Cognitive repairs: How organizational practices can compensate for individual shortcomings. *Research in Organizational Behavior*, 20, 1–37.

Heath, C., and Sitkin, S. (2001). Big-B versus big-O: What is organizational about organizational behavior. *Journal of Organizational Behavior*, 2, 43–58.

Hedström, P., and Swedberg, R. (1996). Social mechanisms. *Acta Sociologica*, 39(3), 281–308.

Heise, D. (1989). Modeling event structures. *Journal of Mathematical Sociology*, 14, 139–69.

Helfat, C. E., and Peteraf, M. A. (2015). Managerial cognitive capabilities and the microfoundations of dynamic capabilities. *Strategic Management Journal*, 36(6), 831–50.

Hendry, J. (2002). The principal's other problems: Honest incompetence and the specification of objectives. *Academy of Management Review*, 27, 98–113.

Hitt, M., Beamish, P., Jackson, S., and Mathieu, J. (2007). Building theoretical and empirical bridges across levels: Multilevel research in management. *Academic Management Journal*, 50, 1385–99.

Hodgson, G. M. (2007). Meanings of methodological individualism. *Journal of Economic Methodology*, 14(2), 211–26.

Hodgson, G. (2012). The mirage of microfoundations. *Journal of Management Studies*, 49, 1389–94.

Hodgson, G., and Knudsen, T. (2011). Poverty of stimulus and absence of cause: Some questions for Felin and Foss. *Journal of Institutional Economics*, 7, 295–8.

Hofmann, D. A., Griffin, M. A., and Gavin, M. B. (2000). The application of hierarchical linear modeling to organizational research, in Klein, K. J., and

Kozlowski, S. W. J. (eds), *Multilevel Theory, Resarch, and Methods in Organizations* San Francisco: Jossey Bass, 467–511.

Holmström, B. (1979). Moral hazard and observability. *The Bell Journal of Economics*, 10(1), 74–91

Homburg, C., Artz, M., and Wieseke, J. (2012). Marketing performance measurement systems: does comprehensiveness really improve performance? *Journal of Marketing*, 76, 56–77.

Hume, D. (1777). *Enquiries concerning Human Understanding and concerning the Principles of Morals, Reprinted from the 1777 edition*, third ed., Nidditch, P. H. (ed.). Oxford: Oxford University Press.

Humphrey, S. E., and LeBreton, J. M. (2019). Introduction, in: Humphrey, S. E., and LeBreton, J. M. (eds), *The Handbook of Multilevel Theory, Measurement, and Analysis*. Washington, DC: American Psychological Association, 3–8.

Hutzschenreuter, T., and Horstkotte, J. (2013). Performance effects of top management team demographic faultlines in the process of product diversification. *Strategic Management Journal*, 34, 704–26.

Jacobides, M. G., and Winter, S. G. (2012). Capabilities: Structure, agency, and evolution. *Organization Science*, 23(5), 1213–522.

James, L. R., and Jones, A. P. (1974). Organizational climate: A review of theory and research. *Psychological Bulletin*, 81, 1096–12.

Janssen, M. (2005). *Microfoundations: A Critical Inquiry*. London: Routledge.

Jebb, A. T., Tay. L., Ng, V., and Woo, S. (2019). Construct validation in multilevel studies, in in: Humphrey, S. E., and LeBreton, J. M. (eds), *The Handbook of Multilevel Theory, Measurement, and Analysis*. Washington, DC: American Psychological Association, 253–78.

Jensen, M. C., and Meckling, W. H. (1976). Theory of the firm: Managerial behavior, agency costs and ownership structure. *Journal of Financial Economics*, 3, 305–60.

Jepperson, R., and Meyer, J. (2011). Multiple levels of analysis and the limitations of methodological individualisms. *Sociological Theory*, 29, 54–73.

Johns, G. (2006). The essential impact of context on organizational behavior. *Academy of Management Review,* 31(2), 386–408.

Johnson, V. (2007). What is organizational imprinting? Cultural entrepreneurship in the founding of the Paris opera. *American Journal of Sociology,* 113, 97–113.

Kaplan, R. S., and Norton, D. P. (1992). The balanced scorecard–measures that drive performance. *Harvard Business Review*, 70(1), 71–9.

Kim, J. Y., Howard, M., Pahnke, E. C., and Boeker, W. (2016). Understanding network formation in strategy research: Exponential random graph models. *Strategic Management Journal*, 37, 22–44.

Kincaid, H. (1997). *Individualism and the Unity of Science: Essays on Reduction, Explanation, and the Special Sciences*. Lanham, MD: Rowman & Littlefield Publishers, Inc.

Klein, K., and Kozlowski, S. (eds) (2000). *Multilevel Theory, Research and Methods in Organizations: Foundations, Extensions and New Directions*. San Francisco: Jossey-Bass, 3–90.

Kogut, B., and Zander, U. (1993). Knowledge of the firm and the evolutionary theory of the multinational corporation. *Journal of International Business Studies*, 24(4), 625–45.

Kozlowski, S., and Klein, K. J. (2000). A multilevel approach to theory and research in organizations: Contextual, temporal, and emergence processes, in Klein, K. J., and Kozlowski, S. W. (eds), *Multilevel Theory, Research and Methods in Organizations: Foundations, Extensions, and New Directions*. San Francisco: Jossey-Bass, 3–90.

Krasikova, D. V., and LeBreton, J. M. (2019). Multilevel measurement: Agreement, reliability, and nonindependence, in Humphrey, S. E., and LeBreton, J. M. (eds), *The Handbook of Multilevel Theory, Measurement, and Analysis*. Washington, DC: American Psychological Association, 279–304.

Lakatos, I. (1970). Falsification and the methodology of scientific research programmes, in Lakatos, I., and Musgrave, A. (eds), *Criticism and the Growth of Knowledge*. New York: Cambridge University Press, 91–196.

Lambsdorff, J. G. (2007). Causes and consequences of corruption: What do we know from a cross-section of countries? in Rose-Ackermann, S. (ed.), *International Handbook on the Economics of Corruption*. Cheltenham: Edward-Elgar Publishing, 3–51

Lewin, A. Y., Massini, S., and Peeters, C. (2011). Microfoundations of internal and external absorptive capacity routines. *Organization Science*, 22, 81–98.

Lewis, D. (1986). Causal explanation, in Lewis, D. (ed.), *Philosophical Papers*, vol. II. Oxford: Oxford University Press, 214–40.

Lindenberg, S., and Foss, N. (2011). Managing joint production motivation: the role of goal framing and governance mechanisms. *Academy of Management Review*, 36, 500–25.

Linder, S., and Foss, N. J. (2018). Microfoundations of organizational goals: A review and new directions for future research. *International Journal of Management Reviews*, 20(S1), S39–S62.

Linder, S., Foss, N. J., and Stea, D. (2017). Epistemics at work: The theory of mind in principal-agent relations, in Hitt, M. A.et al. (eds), *The Oxford Handbook of Strategy Implementation*. Oxford: Oxford University Press, 101–25.

Linder, S., Lyngsie, J., Foss, N. J., and Zahra, S. (2015). Wise choices: How thoroughness of opportunity appraisal, incentives, and performance evaluation fit together. *IEEE Transactions on Engineering Management*, 62(4), 484–94.

Lippman, S. A., and Rumelt, R. P. (2003a). A bargaining perspective on resource advantage. *Strategic Management Journal*, 24, 1069–86.

Lippman, S. A., and Rumelt, R. P. (2003b). The payments perspective: Micro-foundations of resource analysis. *Strategic Management Journal*, 24, 903–27.

Little, D. (1991). *Varieties of Social Explanation: An Introduction to the Philosophy of Social Science*. Boulder, CO: Westview Press.

Little, D. (1998). *Microfoundations, Method, and Causation*. New Brunwick, NJ: Transaction Publishers.

Longford, N. (1986). VARCL – Interactive software for variance component analysis: Applications for survey data. *Professional Statistician*, 5, 28–33.

Longford, N. (1993). *Random Coefficient Models*. New York: Oxford University Press.

Maak, T., Pless, N. M., and Voegtlin, C. (2016). Business statesman or shareholder advocate? CEO responsible leadership styles and the micro-foundations of political CSR. *Journal of Management Studies*, 53, 463–93.

Machamer, P., Darden, L., and Craver, C. F. (2000). Thinking about mechanisms. *Philosophy of Science*, 67, 1–25.

Macy, M. W., and Willer, R. (2002). From factors to actors: Computational sociology and agent-based modeling. *Annual Review of Sociology*, 28, 143–66.

Mäkelä, K., Sumelius, J., Höglund, M., and Ahlvik, C. (2012). Determinants of strategic HR capabilities in MNC subsidiaries. *Journal of Management Studies*, 49, 1459–83.

Malmi, T., and Brown, D. A. (2008). Management control systems as a package –Opportunities, challenges and research directions. *Management Accounting Research*, 19, 287–300.

March, J. (1991). Exploration and exploitation in organizational learning. *Organization Science*, 2, 71–87.

Marschak, J., and Radner, R. (1972). *Economic Theory of Teams*. New Haven, CT: Yale University Press.

Martinkenaite, I., and Breunig, K. J. (2016). The emergence of absorptive capacity through micro–macro level interactions. *Journal of Business Research*, 69, 700–8.

Mathieu, J. E., and Chen, G. (2011). The etiology of the multilevel paradigm in management research. *Journal of Management*, 37(2), 610–41.

Mathieu, J., and Luciano, M. M. (2019). Multilevel emergence in work collectives, in Humphrey, S. E., and LeBreton, J. M. (eds), *The Handbook of Multilevel Theory, Measurement, and Analysis*. Washington, DC: American Psychological Association, 163–86.

Mathieu, J., Maynard, M. T., Rapp, T., and Gilson, L. (2008). Team effectiveness 1997–2007: A review of recent advancements and a glimpse into the future. *Journal of Management*, 34(3), 410–76.

Matten, D., and Moon, J. (2008). 'Implicit' and 'explicit' CSR: A conceptual framework for a comparative understanding of corporate social responsibility. *Academy of Management Review*, 33(2), 404–24.

McKelvey, B., and Andriani, P. (2005). Why Gaussian statistics are mostly wrong for strategic organization. *Strategic Organization*, 3, 219–28.

McWilliams, A., and Siegel, D. (2001). Corporate social responsibility: A theory of the firm perspective. *Academy of Management Review*, 26(1), 117–27.

Menger, C. (1883 [1985]). *Investigations into the Method of the Social Sciences, with Special Reference to Economics*. Schneider, L. (ed.), translated by Francis J. Nock. New York: New York University Press.

Mertens, K. G., Lorscheid, I., and Meyer, M. (2017). Using structural equation-based metamodelling for agent-based models, in Chan, W. K. V., D'Ambrogio, A., Zacharewicz, G., Mustafee, N., Wainer, G., and Page, E. (eds), *Proceedings of the 2017 Winter Simulation Conference*. Washington, DC: IEEE, 1372–82.

Meuer, J., and Rupietta, C. (2017). Integrating QCA and HLM for multilevel research on organizational configurations. *Organizational Research Methods*, 20(2), 324–42.

Milgrom, P., and Roberts, J. (1992). *Economics, Organization and Management*. Englewood Cliffs, NJ: Prentice Hall.

Miller, K. D., Choi, S., and Pentland, B. T. (2014). The role of transactive memory in the formation of organizational routines. *Strategic Organization*, 12(2), 109–33.

Miller, K., Pentland, B., and Choi, S. (2012). Dynamics of performing and remembering organizational routines. *Journal of Management Studies*, 49, 1536–58.

Mollick, E. (2012). People and process, suits and innovators: the role of individuals in firm performance. *Strategic Management Journal*, 33, 1001–15.

Molloy, J. C., Ployhart, R. E., and Wright, P. M. (2011). The myth of 'the' micro-macro divide: Bridging system-level and disciplinary divides. *Journal of Management*, 37, 581–609.

Morris, S., Hammond, R., and Snell, S. (2014). A microfoundations approach to transnational capabilities. *Journal of International Business Studies*, 45, 405–27.

Morris, S. S., Alvarez, S. A., Barney, J. B., and Molloy, J. C. (2017). Firm-specific human capital investments as a signal of general value: Revisiting assumptions about human capital and how it is managed. *Strategic Management Journal*, 38, 912–19.

Münscher, R., Vetter, M., and Scheuerle, T. (2015). A review and taxonomy of choice architecture techniques. *Journal of Behavioral Decision Making*, 29(5), 511–24.

Nelson, R. R., and Winter, S. (1982). *An Evolutionary Theory of Economic Change*. Boston: Harvard University Press.

Nezlek, J. B. (2008). An introduction to multilevel modeling for social and personality psychology. *Social and Personality Psychology Compass*, 2(2), 842–60.

Nickerson, J., and Zenger, T. (2008). Envy, comparison costs, and the economic theory of the firm. *Strategic Management Journal*, 29, 1371–94.

Norman, W., and MacDonald, C. (2004). Getting to the bottom of 'triple bottom line'. *Business Ethics Quarterly*, 14(2), 243–62.

Obloj, T., and Zemsky, P. (2015). Value creation and value capture under moral hazard: Exploring the micro-foundations of buyer–supplier relationships. *Strategic Management Journal*, 36, 1146–63.

Ostroff, C., and Bowen, D. E. (2000). Moving HR to a higher level: HR practices and organizational effectiveness, in Klein, K. J., and Kozlowski, S. W. J. (eds), *Multilevel Theory, Research, and Methods in Organizations*. San Francisco: Jossey-Bass, 211–66.

Paldam, M. (2002). The cross-country pattern of corruption: economics, culture and the seesaw dynamics. *European Journal of Political Economy*, 18(2), 215–40.

Paruchuri, S., and Eisenman, M. (2012). Microfoundations of firm R&D capabilities: A study of inventor networks in a merger. *Journal of Management Studies*, 49, 1509–35.

Pearl, J. (2009). *Causality: Models, Reasoning and Inference*. Cambridge, Cambridge University Press.

Pentland, B. (2011). The (n)ever-changing world: Stability and change in organizational routines. *Organization Science*, 22, 1369–83.

Pentland, B., Feldman, M., Becker, M., and Liu, P. (2012). Dynamics of organizational routines: A generative model. *Journal of Management Studies*, 49, 1484–1508.

Perera Aldama, L., and Zicari, A. (2012). Value-added reporting as a tool for sustainability: A Latin American experience. *Corporate Governance*, 12(4), 485–98.

Peteraf, M. A., and Barney, J. B. (2003). Unravelling the resource-based tangle. *Managerial and Decision Economics*, 24, 309–23.

Ployhart, R. E., and Hendricks, J. (2019). The missing levels in microfoundations, in Humphrey, S. E., and LeBreton, J. M. (eds), *The Handbook of Multilevel Theory, Measurement, and Analysis*. Washington, DC: American Psychological Association, 141–62.

Podsakoff, P. M., MacKenzie, S. B., Lee, J. Y., and Podsakoff, N. P. (2003). Common method biases in behavioral research: A critical review of the literature and recommended remedies. *Journal of Applied Psychology*, 88(5), 879–903.

Porter, M. E. (1979). The structure within industries and companies' performance. *The Review of Economics and Statistics*, 61(2), 214–27.

Powell, T. C., Lovallo, D., and Fox, C. R. (2011). Behavioral strategy. *Strategic Management Journal*, 32, 1369–86.

Raffiee, J., and Coff, R. (2016). Micro-foundations of firm-specific human capital: When do employees perceive their skills to be firm-specific? *Academy of Management Journal*, 59(3), 766–90.

Ragin, C. C. (1987). *The Comparative Method: Moving beyond Qualitative and Quantitative Strategies*. Berkeley: University of California Press.

Ragin, C. C. (1992). 'Casing' and the process of social inquiry, in Ragin, C. C., and Becker, H. S. (eds), *What Is a Case? Exploring the Foundations of Social Inquiry*. Cambridge: Cambridge University Press, 217–26.

Ratzinger-Sakel, N. V., Audousset-Coulier, S., Kettunen, J., and Lesage, C. (2013). Joint Audit: Issues and Challenges for Researchers and Policy-Makers. *Accounting in Europe*, 10(2), 175–99.

Rogan, M., and Mors, M. L. (2014). A network perspective on individual-level ambidexterity in organizations. *Organization Science*, 25(6), 1573–1877.

Rousseau, D. M., and Fried, Y. (2001). Location, location, location: Contextualizing organizational research. *Journal of Organizational Behavior*, 22, 1–13.

Saebi, T., Foss, N. J., and Linder, S. (2019). Social entrepreneurship research: Past achievements and future promises. *Journal of Management*, 45(1), 70–95.

Salvato, C., and Rerup, C. (2018). Routine regulation: Balancing conflicting goals in organizational routines. *Administrative Science Quarterly*, 63(1), 170–209.

Satz, D., and Ferejohn, J. (1994). Rational choice and social theory. *The Journal of Philosophy*, 91(2), 71–87.

Scherer, F. (1980). *Industrial Market Structure and Economic Performance*, second ed. Skokie, IL: Rand McNally College Publishing Company.

Serra, D. (2011). Combining top-down and bottom-up accountability: Evidence from a bribery experiment. *The Journal of Law, Economics, & Organization*, 28(3), 569–87.

Silberstein, M. D. (2002). Reduction, emergence and explanation, in Machamer, P., and Silberstein, M. (eds), *The Blackwell Guide to the Philosophy of Science*. Oxford: Blackwell Publishers Ltd.

Simon, H. A. (1955). A behavioral model of rational choice. *Quarterly Journal of Economics*, 69, 99–118.

Simon, H. (1961). *Administrative Behavior*. New York: The Free Press.

Spender, J.-C. (1996). Making knowledge the basis of a dynamic theory of the firm. *Strategic Management Journal*, 17, 45–62.

Spirtes, P., Glymour, C., and Scheines, R. S. (2000). *Causation, Prediction, and Search*. New York: Springer-Verlag.

Staats, B. R., Milkman, K. L., and Fox, C. R. (2012). The team scaling fallacy: Underestimating the declining efficiency of larger teams. *Organizational Behavior and Human Decision Processes*, 118, 132–42.

Steidlmeier, P. (1999). Gift giving, bribery and corruption: Ethical management of business relationships in China. *Journal of Business Ethics*, 20(2), 121–32.

Stinchcombe, A. L. (1965). Social structure and organizations, in March, J. G. (ed.), *Handbook of Organizations*. New York: Rand McNally, 142–93.

Stirling, W. C., and Felin, T. (2013). Game theory, conditional preferences and social influence. *PLoS ONE*, 8(2), e56751.

Strauss, K., Lepoutre, J., and Wood, G. (2017). Fifty shades of green: How microfoundations of sustainability dynamic capabilities vary across organizational contexts. *Journal of Organizational Behavior*, 38, 1338–55.

Sugden, R. (2016). Ontology, methodological individualism, and the foundations of the social sciences. *Journal of Economic Literature*, 54(4), 1377–89.

Sunder, S., and Gode, D. (1993). Allocative efficiency of markets with zero-intelligence traders: Market as a partial substitute for individual rationality. *Journal of Political Economy*, 101(1), 119–37.

Teece, D. (2007). Explicating dynamic capabilities: The nature and microfoundations of (sustainable) enterprise performance. *Strategic Management Journal*, 28, 1319–50.

Thaler, R. H., and Sunstein, C. (2008). *Nudge: Improving Decisions about Health, Wealth and Happiness*. New Haven, CT: Yale University Press.

Thornton, P. H., Ocasio, W., and Lounsbury, M. (2012). *The Institutional Logics Perspective: A New Approach to Culture, Structure and Process*. Oxford: Oxford University Press.

Tuncdogan, A., Boon, A., Mom, T., van den Bosch, F., and Volberda, H. (2017). Management teams' regulatory foci and organizational units' exploratory innovation: The mediating role of coordination mechanisms. *Long Range Planning*, 50, 621–35.

Udehn, L. (2001). *Methodological Individualism: Background, History and Meaning*. London: Routledge.

Udehn, L. (2002). The changing face of methodological individualism. *Annual Review of Sociology*, 28, 479–507.

Venkatesh, V., Brown, S. A., and Bala, H. (2013). Bridging the qualitative-quantitative divide: Guidelines for conducting mixed methods research in information systems. *MIS Quarterly*, 37(1), 21–54.

Weintraub, E. R. (1979). *Microfoundations: The Compatibility of Microeconomics and Macroeconomics*. Cambridge, MA: Cambridge University Press.

Wernerfelt, B. (1984). A resource-based view of the firm. *Strategic Management Journal*, 5, 171–80.

Whetten, D., Felin, T., and King, B. (2009). The practice of theory borrowing in organizational studies: Current issues and future directions. *Journal of Management*, 35, 537–63.

Wilden, R., Devinney, T. M., and Dowling, G. R. (2016). The architecture of dynamic capability research: Identifying the building blocks of a configurational approach. *Academy of Management Annals*, 10, 997–1076.

Williamson, O. E. (1985). *The Economic Institutions of Capitalism*. New York: The Free Press.

Williamson, O. E. (1996). Efficiency, power, authority and economic organization, in Groenewegen, J. (ed.),*Transaction Cost Economics and Beyond*. New York, Springer, 11–43.

Winter, S. G. (2011). Problems at the foundation? Comments on Felin and Foss. Journal of *Institutional Economics*, 7, 257–77.

Winter, S. G. (2012a). Capabilities: Their origins and ancestry. *Journal of Management Studies*, 49, 1402–6.

Winter, S. G. (2012b). Purpose and progress in the theory of strategy: Comments on Gavetti. *Organization Science*, 23, 1213–26.

Winter, S. G. (2013). Habit, deliberation and action: Strengthening the micro-foundations of routines and capabilities. *Academy of Management Perspectives*, 27(2), 120–37.

Wright, P., Coff, R., and Moliterno, T. (2014). Strategic human capital: Crossing THE Great divide. *Journal of Management*, 14, 353–70.

Yao, F. K., and Chang, S. (2017). Do individual employees' learning goal orientation and civic virtue matter? A micro-foundations perspective on firm absorptive capacity. *Strategic Management Journal*, 38, 2041–60.

Zerni, M., Haapamäki, E., Järvinen, T., and Niemi, L. (2012). Do joint audits improve audit quality? Evidence from voluntary joint audits. *European Accounting Review*, 21(4), 731–65.

Cambridge Elements ≡

Business Strategy

J.-C. Spender
Rutgers Business School
J.-C. Spender is a visiting scholar at Rutgers Business School and a research Professor, Kozminski University. He has been active in the business strategy field since 1971 and is the author or co-author of 7 books and numerous papers. His principal academic interest is in knowledge-based theories of the private sector firm, and managing them.

About the Series
Business strategy's reach is vast, and important too since wherever there is business activity there is strategizing. As a field, strategy has a long history from medieval and colonial times to today's developed and developing economies. This series offers a place for interesting and illuminating research including industry and corporate studies, strategizing in service industries, the arts, the public sector, and the new forms of Internet-based commerce. It also covers today's expanding gamut of analytic techniques.

Cambridge Elements $^{=}$

Business Strategy

Elements in the Series

Printed in the United States
By Bookmasters